Personal Assistant

"A Servant's Heart"

Guidelines for Women Serving God's Leaders

by

Deborah D. Vereen

In Praise of *A Servant's Heart*

"I think it is fair to say we live in a world where most people want to be up front, in charge, and take the lead rather than discovering the immense power, joy and satisfaction associated with learning to serve the individual who is the leader of a group.

Early in my ministry, I was called to serve as Special Assistant to the Pastor of a large Congregation in New York City. Fresh out of seminary, I was convinced God had called me not to serve as a lead or senior pastor. On the contrary, I knew God had called me to serve as the personal assistant to a senior pastor.

God had given me the spiritual insight to see the enormous responsibility and the enormous burden that the senior minister of a large congregation faced and I felt God calling me to serve God's people by assisting the Lead Pastor. Since I was theologically trained and ordained to serve in professional ministry, I knew God had given me a unique opportunity to serve the Senior Minister of a local congregation in ways that a layperson could not serve.

As I sought to serve faithfully in the place where God had placed me, I began to experience a number of personal challenges. These challenges eventually led me to question my calling, question my self-esteem and at times question my personal values and convictions. An incomplete and inadequate understanding of the ministry of a personal assistant drove these questions.

This book is a must for any person interested in understanding how and why God calls some of us to serve as personal assistants to others who provide leadership to the community of faith. After reflecting theologically on being called as a Personal Assistant, Pastor Vereen provides practical guidelines to help Personal Assistants serve confidently and effectively.

In retrospect, I wish I had at my disposal a book like this. The insights contained in Pastor Vereen's thoughts and research would have spared me a number of restless nights, many tears, and the doubts regarding my self-esteem, values and convictions. In short, I suffered because of a lack of knowledge".

—**William B. Sutton, III, D. Min., Princeton Theological Seminary;** Senior Pastor, The Historic First Baptist Church of Stratford; Immediate Past President, American Baptist

Churches of Connecticut (ABCCONN); Chairperson, Board of Directors, *So Send I You* – A Foreign Missions Initiative President, Stratford Clergy Association

"Who can be saved? God saves us when we answer His call. If you have a feeling that God is calling you to serve, pray first. This book is a guide that helps women seriously to practice their faith when God calls. Many women are called, but few respond. If you feel the urge to serve, pray first to discover if this is God calling. As you read, you will find helpful means of answering the call of God. Record in a journal your thoughts and ideas about the helpful clues to becoming a server for God. Then put your response from God to good faithful use. Be blessed as much as the author continues to be blessed. In prayer, pray for Deborah who took a leap of faith to write this to m".

—Reverend DeOla Barfield, Deacon; MS

"To write from the heart is an accomplishment many people only dream of, but Pastor Deborah Vereen has achieved that in her book that could easily have the sub-title, "The Servant's Heart." Written with the intimate knowledge of a traveler who "knows the road," she tackles the subject of serving as it relates specifically to those in authority, especially the "Pastor's wife." It is not a book that is meant to be read as fantasy, fiction or history. It is written in a way that those in leadership can appreciate as well as those seeking God's direction in specific and challenging roles. Anyone who wants to experience a deeper level of joy as they "serve" God's "servants " will want to read this book and keep it close by as a reference, guide and source of encouragement as they fulfill the Lord's plan for their life".
        —**Jeanette Harris** (performance artist, author, singer, songwriter)

Deborah D. Vereen
Mercy Tabernacle Church
P.O. Box 22
Stratford, Connecticut 06615
pastordeborahdvereen@yahoo.com

Printed in the United States of America.
The text of this book is set in Lucinda Bright
The display face is Lucinda Bright

King James Version of The Bible has been used.

This title is registered with The Library of Congress.

Ordering Information:
Quantity sales. Special discounts are available on quantity purchases by corporations, associations, and others. For details, contact the author at the address above.

ISBN: 978-0-6923-2940-5

Contents

Acknowledgments

All Glory Honor and Praise Belongs to God, The Father, Creator of everything. I know without Him I could do nothing, but with him I can do all things.

To my husband and friend Woodrow:
Woodrow, you have been my #1 supporter, encourager and most definitely the greatest inspiration in my spiritual walk. You are a "Great Man of God" well respected and a "Man of Integrity". You've ministered to my needs and encouraged me through the rough times. Thank you love for always being right by my side. You are the greatest Husband, Dad and friend. Thanks for believing in me and for all your support, patience, understanding and most of all your love which we have shared for 33 years with more to come. I'm proud and honored to be your wife. "I Love you" Deb

To my wonderful children: LaKeya, Woodrow Jr., (Shabiroon) Travis (Madeline), Kevin (Shabriyah) and Loretta, I am so proud to be your mom and I love you all so very much. My special grandchildren: Keziah, Josai, Niyanna, Jaxon, Aubree and Adjatay! I love you all.

In Loving memory of my late father Anderson Stevenson (January 4 2013) and late mother Hattie Stevenson (December 21, 2013) who I loved dearly; they will always be in my heart. To my siblings who supported me down through the years.

Bishop John C. White, Pastor and Presiding Prelate of Cathedral of Praise C.O.G.I.C. International. First Lady, Elder Gloria White, the woman of God whom God called me to serve. I and am yet privileged to continue assisting for more than 20 years. I thank God for the call and for choosing me to serve you. Sister White, my sincere love. Thank you, Cathedral of Praise!

Betty Lawson a dear friend and woman of God. Thank you for assisting my children as I did the work of the Lord. You have truly supported me and my family as I traveled, thank you for being the "Nanny".

Prophet Christopher Bruce for the confirmation of this book.

Apostle Tom and Prophetess Kathy Lounsbury, Apostle Bobby Gardner and Pastor Mary Gardner, thank you for your open arms and your open doors. You've shown so much love to me.

Mercy Tabernacle Church of which I am Co-Pastor - thank you for your love, prayers and support.

Special Thanks

Reverend DeOla Barfield, Deacon; MS
Minister Tracey Criss
Maggie Pate Duffey
Jeanette Harris
Shannon Healey
Deborah Perry
Sylvia Scott
Lakeya Stevenson
Loretta Vereen
Shabiroon Vereen

Prayer Partners
Elder Velma Greenlee
Minister Veronica Johnson
Mary Morris
Elder Linda Somerville

Personal Assistants
Sister Betty Smith
Evangelist Kristina Stevenson

Dedication

I would like to dedicate this book to my late mother, Mrs. Hattie Mae Stevenson, December 12, 2013 at 8:21 pm. So vividly, I'm holding your hand, saying a prayer and tears streaming down my face, you went from labor to reward taking your last breath on earth into eternity. Mom, I will always hold you in my memories and most especially in my heart; yes, I've often told you and others that you were my best friend and hero. Born November 1924, in Mississippi during the time of segregation, you allowed God to use the gifts and talents of serving others without reservation. Even though you did not have the opportunity to graduate high school or even attend junior high, your wisdom was so profound. God gave you the words to say and things just happened for the best! Sharing her love, passion and compassion as the eldest, you assisted your mother in raising your siblings.

Mom nurtured, cultivated, demonstrated love and served her family without limits. As a child, I remember the love she shared with each of us equally.

To you, Mom, I *dedicate* this book. To you, Mom, I give you praise for the values that you instilled in me and the love that was exemplified throughout my life. Untiringly you prayed, made sacrifices and gave of yourself not only to your biological family but extended family, friends and even those you did not know personally.

I recall many conversations with my mom and these are a few that stand out. She would always share how she loved all the children the same. How she would give her last to be sure our needs were met. She would talk about education and encourage us to excel and be all that we could. She would tell us to work hard; not be lazy; value life, value our family; go to church and love God. She would say treat people right; help those that you can and God will bless you. She would talk about the Lord and how good He was to her and how she had joy in telling someone everyday about Him. My mother was one of a kind! I truly believe that today I am who I am and what I am because of the many things she has taught me as a child especially when it comes to putting others first.

It all began here for me as a youngster, going where she went, watching what she would do and listening to what she would say. I'd go with her to different locations so that I could assist with preparing the meals and serve the families. Sometimes there would be a hundred to two hundred people depending on the person whose life had came to an end. On other occasions we would prepare the food at home, take it to the facility, serve the families, clean the facility and then go home. We were there sometimes three to five hours, setting up the place, chair, and tables.

I remember watching and learning how to serve, but didn't fully understand that my gifts from the Lord were be cultivated and nurtured by the one and only Mama. As God gave her instructions and guidance I was also being groomed. I can literally say, I sat at her feet. I've witnessed those bound with afflictions and addictions set free. Yes it was intense as some addicted to drugs would literally go cold turkey, cold sweats, shakes, nodding there on the couch with stuff coming out their mouth and nose; it was a sight to see; others wounded she would bound up the wounds so they would live and not die; yes she served as a physician without anesthesia. Let me include the emotionally challenged and those turned away because of their lifestyles. My mother was right there determined to help I was right beside her.

Seeing the things my mother did gave me a personal desire to do the same, and much of it I did. Now married for thirty-three years, my husband and I have opened our home from the first year of our marriage as a safe haven until the present. I watched my mom sew and I would practice making doll clothes and then as a young adult make hats and scarves and give them away. I also enjoy cooking big meals and feeding people as she did.

I'd like to say to you, dear reader, that the gift of our service is truly a gift not to withhold. Many are in need today. I found sharing and caring not only satisfied others but will give you such a gratifying feeling. Just knowing someone who was hungry is no longer hungry, someone who was cold has shelter, someone who needs a helping hand has ours and someone who needs a shoulder to lean on can come to you.

My mom served her community as a former Father Panik Village Tenants Association President. She was instrumental in opening and operating a licensed sandwich shop. As a devoted Christian she distributed bread and non-perishable foods throughout her community and I was right there with her helping out. My mother was a phenomenal woman! Everyone who came in contact with her loved her. When she would enter the grocery store, Blacks, Hispanics and Caucasians would all say, "Hi Mama, what you need? Is everything alright? Let me pay for that." The store-owner would ask, "How many children do you have?" She would reply, "They are all my children." Her unconditional love exuberated throughout the community and her home was a safe haven for many. As I stated, my home has been a safe haven for many as well. Indeed, she was a great inspiration and a great leader who was thoughtful, caring and unselfish. People from all walks of life would come and sit at our table and eat. Oh, the food was scrumptious! Fried chicken, sweet potatoes, collard greens, mac and cheese, potato salad and corn bread.

My mom was a woman on a mission with a vision. She was a woman to behold. She wore many hats, her mind was always ticking and those hands were always busy. She would always say, "I just have to tell someone about Jesus every day." Her passion was to win souls to the Kingdom of God by sharing the good news and helping others faithfully. She was a spiritual leader in the community who practiced what she preached. She gave godly counsel and imparted much knowledge to those she came in contact with. Her love was priceless; she helped raise a community, as her home was a place of refuge for the sick, hungry and homeless. She did not point her finger, but instead, she held out her loving hands and helped everyone including those she didn't know. She gave tender love and care along with a prayer of faith. Yes, my mom was a praying woman who looked to Jesus for daily strength and guidance.

My mother prayed and believed and God answered many of her prayers. I was her first child of fourteen siblings to become a Christian, Missionary, Minister, Evangelist, and Co-Pastor.

With respect to my mother's vision and dream, I plan to keep alive her legacy of love and servitude. I thank her for teaching me little can become much when you put it in the right hands. In the hand of almighty God I place this book trusting that others will glean and learn that we are truly helpers of one another. Lastly, I thank her for supporting me as I preached at various churches and for confirming that my husband Pastor Woodrow of thirty-three years would be my husband. I await the day when we are reunited by the resurrection power of God.

From the depths of my soul, I thank her for all that she has taught me especially how to give of myself and not be selfish and how to live a life that would please the Lord. I praise God for her trusting me, as she would often say, "Miss", I trust you with my life.

In honor of my mom, with sincere love, I dedicate this book to her and give her praise for being a "Virtuous Woman of God". I LOVE YOU!

Eternal love,

"Missy"

This dedication is to my beloved Mom - Mother Hattie Stevenson

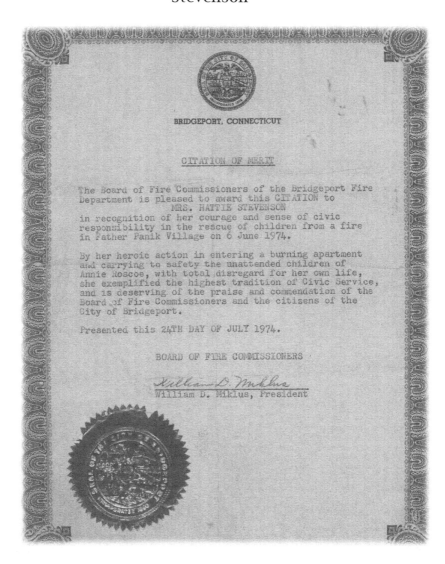

BRIDGEPORT, CONNECTICUT

CITATION OF MERIT

The Board of Fire Commissioners of the Bridgeport Fire Department is pleased to award this CITATION to
MRS. HATTIE STEVENSON
in recognition of her courage and sense of civic responsibility in the rescue of children from a fire in Father Panik Village on 6 June 1974.

By her heroic action in entering a burning apartment and carrying to safety the unattended children of Annie Roscoe, with total disregard for her own life, she exemplified the highest tradition of Civic Service, and is deserving of the praise and commendation of the Board of Fire Commissioners and the citizens of the City of Bridgeport.

Presented this 24TH DAY OF JULY 1974.

BOARD OF FIRE COMMISSIONERS

William D. Miklus, President

Introduction

I'm reminiscing, I'm excited and I'm delighted to share with you the assignment God called me to fulfill. I'm sure you're inquisitive to know because this book is in your hand, so please allow me to share from my heart the greatness of God and the awesome experiences he allotted me.

I'm privileged and honored to have been called to serve and assist one of God's women in the body of Christ for over twenty years. I've witnessed the need for us "women" to put aside our personal agendas and embrace each other with love, as we share and care for one another.

I'm not writing from another man's script or experiences but from a personal perspective on the true need of women to be loyal, faithful and honest as they share in ministry and no longer be competitive. Trust me on this - God has need of you, because there is a definite lack of support for the women in the body of Christ. Are you the one who will be willing to allow God to use you?

All around us are women who must be willing to challenge themselves to stop being oppositional, critical, judgmental and face the facts that we truly need each other.

Serving and assisting is an awesome task; one can't do it without the other, so let's work together. Let's agree to disagree; to stop minimizing our sister's talent and gifts but only try to maximize ourselves.

Let's become more sensitive to the needs and allow God to use us to minister healing and provide strength and support the Pastors, Prophetess, Evangelist, Ministers, who have been called to preach and teach the gospel and those who need us. Remember serving is a ministry and we can't limit this to those only in ministry.

Jesus said he came to serve and not to be served. Are you willing to adapt and adjust to serve and assist when and where necessary? Do you see the vision? We are one! It's truly time for us all to realize ministry is not about "me" "myself" and "I" it's about "us". We are helpers, one of the other!

If you presently assist or plan to assist in any of these capacities, Personal Assistant, Adjutant or Armor bearer, this book will motivate you.

Contained in the pages forthcoming you'll engage in some explicit and integral details on the functions of assisting and serving, aiding and helping other women; Oh yes, a wealth of gems and treasures that will last a lifetime.

This book has been in the making for a long time and I give all glory, honor, and praise to God for allowing it to come to fruition.

As you pick up the book you'll be encouraged to fulfill God's plan and purpose for your life. Deborah declares she never could have made it without making a commitment to the Lord Jesus Christ, knowing he is the only one who could fulfill all of his blessings and promises.

Chapter One

Here I Am Lord. Use Me!

In August of 1991, the Lord spoke to me and said, *"I want you to serve Sister White. Do whatever you can to help her."*

I thought to myself " Okay Lord", but I was unsure of exactly what her needs were and how I would be of assistance. I continued to pray and waited for the Lord to speak again and He did.

Upon hearing for the second time *"the call"* from the Lord, I sat down with my husband, Woodrow, and shared what had been put in my heart. Without reservation Woodrow said, "Deb, do it! Talk to Sister White and let her know what God said. Then do what you do best – serve others with love and joy. God has blessed you with these gifts. Go ahead with His blessings and my full support."

I was excited yet somewhat hesitant because I had not served in this capacity before and I didn't know her on a personal level. My heart and spirit were ready but my mind and body were hesitant because I didn't know how it would be received.

I watched Sister White from a distance, and I got the impression that she was somewhat of a private person. She appeared quiet and reserved, a woman of few words who was very mature in her walk with the Lord. I noticed that certain people would gravitate to her after church but that she did not go about talking to everyone in the room.

After service one Sunday morning, I finally got up the nerve to walk up to her and asked if could I speak with her privately. I followed her upstairs to her office and there we sat looking at each other, smiling not knowing what one was going to say to the other. I took a deep breath and let it out. We looked at each other, chuckled and smiled. Then I began to share with her what the Lord had put in my heart. I also expressed my hesitation in coming to her with this calling, afraid of not being understood. But I opened my heart to her and told her what the Lord had asked of me.

Lady White stared at me and thought quietly. Then she said, "Serve me." "But I'm nobody" She shook her head and said, "I ain't nobody special. Before you, Sister Missy no one had helped me in the ministry so I don't know what to expect or where to begin either except to say to you, Sister Missy, if the Lord told you to help me, then it's okay with me. We'll have to learn together."

But she was a smart woman and asked grounded questions. "Are you sure about this?" she asked. "What about your husband and your family? Don't you have small children?"

My husband and I have discussed this in depth, "I responded", and we have always said we would not hinder one another from doing what the Lord asks us to do within the ministry from the beginning of our marriage. Trust me. I will not neglect my first priority, which is my husband and my family. Woodrow and I made a commitment to work for the Lord as a team. Woodrow gives me his support. Woodrow and I have established our priority with God being first. Our marriage and family come next and then the ministry within the church."

"Glory be to God!" Lady White shouted. "Okay!" Everything wasn't set in stone as it was a first for the two of us, but I made a commitment to God that I would serve her to the best of my ability with his help. I refuse to give God haphazard service. It's all the way or no way. Although this was a first for me to serve a first lady, I took pride in it. I recall the day we spoke. It is so very vivid, seems like yesterday. Now over twenty years have passed and we are still working together in the ministry. Hallelujah!!

Prior to my serving First Lady White, she had had three great women who were travelling with her; Auntie Jackie Dominick, Minister Autry Ashley and Sister Ruth Costen. Unfortunately, prior to the beginning of my assignment, Sister Ruth Costen was called to her eternal home. Auntie Jackie Dominick and Minister Autry Ashley welcomed me with open arms. When I would travel with them they didn't know I felt intimidated. They were some anointed women. They loved the Word and talked about it all day. They watched the Word channels 24-7! I thought to myself,"Isn't something else on?" but I didn't dare turn the channel. I felt so blessed and honored to sit and learn from them. They weren't about foolishness. They weren't competitive but *confident* in their walk with the Lord.

I'd sit and listen to them talk to each other expressing their opinions without opposition and ill feelings. Yes, they had differences of opinion, but it didn't ruin their relationships. As I often say, it's okay to agree to disagree. They were versatile, diverse, and competent and it was all good. I really enjoyed being in their company. They laughed, shared experiences and enjoyed each other.

A few years after my service began, we all had a chance to meet up again when I drove Sister White to

Virginia. Auntie Jackie, Sister Ashley, Sister White and I stayed at a hotel directly across the street from Virginia Beach. We had such a good time. We walked the broad walk, shopped and ate.

As time went on, they handed me the car key saying, "Here Sister Missy. You drive." What an experience! Everything just began to fall into place. I began driving, attending to Lady White's personal needs, making her announcement to the appropriate person upon arrival, carrying her garments, assisting her with dressing, as well as praying and assisting her on the pulpit. Auntie Jackie and Sister Ashley would go in the church and be seated.

Sister White is a preaching machine and everyone loves to hear her. The churches treated her with such respect and honor and the people were very receptive to the Word. Listening to her preach was a joy! Certainly my strength was being renewed time and time again.

Some of our places of worship were New York, New Jersey, Maryland, Washington, D.C., Richmond, Virginia, Raleigh, North Carolina, as well as in the Connecticut area.

Time and season are both important because it wasn't long before both Minister Ashley and Auntie Jackie relocated. By this time I had a little experience under my belt. I remained diligent, faithful, consistent, determined, steadfast and unmovable, persistent, and resilient in performing my work for the Lord. God knew what it would take and He equipped me. Being faithful and committed were not optional, but a must.

Prior to Auntie Jackie departing, she gave me her final instructions one Sunday as we sat in T.F.T. Sanctuary. Her look was one of absolute seriousness as she said to me, "Sister Missy, take care of my friend. I'm trusting you. Take care of Glo, don't let anything happen to her. "I assured her that I was going to do this. That small conversation set the tone and from then until now, she has not had to worry about Sister White. Auntie knew that I said what I meant and so did Sister White.

In the Old Testament, the armor bearer would literally kill if the person they served were in danger with no questions asked. I didn't have to go to that extreme. However, there were some that I did have to approach from time to time. It's best said like this: When needed, I would be her voice and do whatever was necessary on her behalf. When she thought the thought, I could see it on her face and feel it in her spirit. I would take care of the situation and inform her that everything was ok.

The seeds in my life were planted in good soil and the fruit of love, joy, peace, patience, kindness, goodness, faithfulness, gentleness, self-control were well established. I understood whom I was serving – God. I had to act appropriately because I was accountable to Him. Yet I was always sure to get the matter resolved.

Working in such close proximately with the First Lady, or the person you are serving, can become difficult. Keeping friendship and your work separate is key. My first priority was not to be a friend, but to fulfill the call of God by assisting her in every aspect. At one point I had a hard time and told her of my concern "being in too deep". She asked, "What does that mean?" I said, "You remember that old song, 'I'm Stuck in the Bucket and I Can't Get Out'? "Attachment", an attachment is a feeling that binds one to a person, thing, cause, ideal or the like; devotion or regard. The synonyms are love, devotedness and connection as with a true sister or friend." I constantly reminded myself this is a call from God, this was not about friendship it was about a work that needed to be completed.

I thank God that although we didn't agree on everything, the Word took precedence and our personal differences were kept minimal. Through our travels, I learned more about the type of person she was and most importantly I learned a lot about myself. I went through some drastic changes and the most rewarding lesson that I learned was acceptance - accepting her for who she was. I have to tell you, it was a bit of a challenge. Diversity is a good thing and we shared and learned from each other.

Different? Did I say different? Sister White and I were *so* different. I guess she thought I was truly a "piece of work", but the truth is, God was working on *both of us.* She could be "short" with me, but not rude or obnoxious. She could sit there and I would talk and she would tune me out. It really irked me in the beginning, but guess what? I dealt with it and conquered it. I simply studied her expressions so that I knew when to speak, how long to speak. All of us need to work on ourselves and not on the other person. We all need to realize our way is not the only way. What might be okay for you will not work for them or vice versa.

As travelling partners we were so different in character, yet we embraced one another's differences. I really respected that in all of those women. I recall hearing years ago that some people are hard to get along with and some you don't want to be bothered with. But to see these women in action simply blew my mind. I thought "Wow! I am not sure if I can do it, but I am willing to try."

I spent countless hours and valuable moments with Lady White and allowed God to cultivate and develop me with his character and humility so that I would serve with the God given gifts and abilities.

Some people are aware of their abilities yet they have to be nurtured, cultivated and developed so that God could get the glory. I realize that all that I am and all that I do is a result of the God who lives in me. To serve others is not as easy as it seems.

This ability comes from God. I realized serving was a honor and privilege. It was not for my personal gratification or my own exclusive enjoyment but in order to help others. We must practice using our gifts, talents and abilities for God. Use them to help, serve, assist as he leads, guides and directs. We must remember to be faithful until our time of serving is done and always lean and depend on the Lord for his direction.

So over the years, Sister White and I traveled far and near. I'd drive and sing or we would chit-chat. She would read her Word then take a snooze until we arrived at our destination. I laugh now because they say couples are drawn together because they are so different. I found this to be the same way. We were able to complement one another in our personalities. We were made of different stock but together we were a team. Her maturity as a Christian, mother, wife and first lady helped me to grow in many areas of my life. I didn't know then that it was a set up by God Himself in preparation for my ministry.

Looking back it seemed as if we had nothing in common, yet God strategically put us together with a plan and a purpose. She was laid back and reserved and was more of an introvert. I was a feisty little something, like Peter, ready to cut off someone's ear! Lady White would call me, she would say, "Sister Missy!!" I would reply, "Sister White, she/he best not get it twisted because you would have to rescue me from what I was about to do. I will protect you but you have to be willing to bail me out!"

Sister White is a woman with a lot of wisdom and it benefited me to listen, whether she spoke in a crowd or directly to me. I confess it wasn't always easy but I took advantage of the opportunity in doing right even when I didn't want to. I am not telling you that I passed every test but I made progress by relying on God's power and strength and not my own. I'm not trying to project to you a picture of me being holier than Thou. It was a struggle and some battles I won, some I lost. Yet, I did continue to follow in my heart what I felt were the right things, always asking the Lord to help me.

In some instances I felt justified in what I wanted to say or do. But for the most part, I held back and tried to weigh the costs and consider the consequences of my actions ahead of time, because there were times I was ready to just fight it out!

People have a tendency to take you where you don't want to go! Boy, I had my moments! In all that, I still thought that I would rather please God and not bring shame to Him. I had choices and so do you. The choice is that you can listen to yourself or listen to God.

Of course, it is just natural to defend yourself, isn't it? But when I gave in to "self", I repented. Often times we react in our flesh and must learn to be led by the spirit. Our tongues are like fire. While they seem to be such a little member, they can be a weapon of mass destruction. As the saying goes, "every thought is not expedient to be spoken!" Ouch! Oftentimes she would say to me, "Girl, you are something else, (a mess). Yea, you are from the ghetto! "

I would tell her that I have to keep (Missy-the ghetto village girl under control) and allow (Deborah) the Christian Woman to have dominance. I was extroverted, fun, loud, outgoing, assertive, yet sensitive to people, sociable and hospitable, but I didn't like nonsense. My motto was "zero tolerance for the nonsense".

I didn't participate in gossip. It was known that I was friendly, loving and kind but my meekness was not a weakness. I was confident of who I was and that kind of irked people. We all prejudge and sometimes I was misunderstood and misjudged and I have done the same to others. But again, no matter how hard, I couldn't ignore what God said to do, but let me tell you sisters, *it took work. I had to work on me!* Unhappy people tend not to like you because they might want to do what you are doing. My attitude was "do it. I am doing what I was called to do so as long as you don't cross over, we're fine." Oftentimes, we try to justify our actions. The Bible says every man is right in his own eyes. The secret is that discipline and self-control are necessities in order to serve.

Many first ladies are so busy assisting their husbands in his ministry that they fail to develop their own ministry and utilize their gifts. My prayer is that every woman of God seizes the moment to fulfill God's purpose. I truly praise God that Elder Gloria White, who, by the leading of the Lord, went forth proclaiming the Word of God. Through her ministry my life has been enriched. I'm grateful that God choose me to serve her. This God-fearing woman is a woman of integrity. She is the wife of Bishop John C. White. She is the 1st Pastoral Assistant at The Cathedral of Praise, National Mother for the Church of God In Christ International, Nationwide Evangelist and Psalmist of the former Institutional Radio Choir Brooklyn, New York and the J.C. White Singers. She attended Manhattan Bible Institute and completed a course in Biblical Studies. She holds a certificate of completion for external courses through Rhema Bible School in Tulsa, Oklahoma. She has several certificates, awards and trophies marking her progression in the call to Christian service. Presently, she is working untiringly with her husband, Bishop White, to bring to fruition the vision given by God - a senior citizen's complex, rehabilitation center for ex-offenders, an orphanage, day care center and a school where young people can learn the ways of the Lord which is vital to their destiny, along with the necessary academics. She is the mother of five children and the grandmother of ten. Sister White loves the Lord Jesus Christ and presses on to know him more, as it is through the knowledge of Him we have all things that pertain to life and Godliness.

It took a lot of humility on her part in allowing me to serve her. I thank her because I would not have ascertained such wisdom, knowledge, experience, training and personal growth if she had not been in agreement. I thank her for helping me in my spiritual makeover and for her patience and prayers for me. I am forever grateful for her generous love and support.

Many women in ministry travel alone. We need to make ourselves available for traveling and be willing to pray, encourage, strengthen and undergird these women. We need to join in as one body together, not envious or jealous, not competitive but to compliment. We need each other for support. Be faithful women of God to this calling and God will be faithful to you. There will be many opportunities to share and embrace thoughts and ideas. Stay open to hear and receive. Remain steadfast under pressure. Become an intercessor and seek the Lord daily, listening attentively to the voice of God. I just want to encourage you to serve with a pure heart and a good conscience. Have you noticed most male Pastors have adjutants and assistants but when you see the wife she's walking in alone. I encourage all of you to offer yourself as an assistant to undergird and meet the needs of the woman of God who assists, undergirds and meets the need of the man of God.

We have some very prominent women in this 21st century in need of an "Assistant." Can she depend on you? Women in ministry are women of integrity, women of faith, women who are willing to make sacrifices. They are praying women who undergird and support the ministry. These are not women who are busy bodies who are in other people's business.

Not all of the women you serve will be the wife of a pastor. She may be the pastor, prophetess, elder, deacon, evangelist, or teacher, but she needs you. Time is of the essence and we must not continue to forsake those who need us. The details of accompanying them will be later discussed as there are many aspects of assisting. As for now, love one another, pray for the gift of discerning spirits and pray for yourself.

God called me. She didn't ask nor did I just wake up one morning and decide I wanted to volunteer as her assistant. Knowing this, kept me moving forward in my responsibility even when the enemy would use whosoever he could to sow seeds of discord or to cause some misunderstanding. My desire was to be the best assistant. I went to God for direction on what to do and what not to do. I also asked for her advice, concerns and suggestions, after which I made some personal changes. I didn't make all the right choices and decisions, but I did learn from the experiences. As an assistant, try not to be over assertive but sensitive, humble, and submissive with a positive attitude.

In the chapters ahead there's insight from my personal journey of how I was led to serve as armor bearer, adjutant and personal assistant I am in no way indicating this is the only way, but there are some good gems you'll be able to glean to help you along the way. I'm praying that we avail ourselves to undergird, strengthen, support and assist in the capacity that is required as we proclaim the word of the Lord.

Chapter 3

Yes Lord, I Will:
Reflections on Chapters 1 and 2

Here you will find a guide to aid you in the process of answering the call of God and allowing God to consecrate you for His purpose. Afterward, there is a questionnaire for you to review the first three chapters of this guide. Think and pray on these things.

1. The Call to Salvation is for All.

> **For God so loved the world that He gave his only begotten son that whosoever believeth in him should not perish but have everlasting life, for God sent not his son into the world to condemn the world but that the world through him might be saved.**
> **(John 3:16)**

2. Respond to the Call with an emphatic "YES!"

> **The word is nigh thee even in thy mouth, that if thou shall confess with thy mouth the Lord Jesus and believe in Thine heart that God has raised him from the dead thou shall be saved, for with the mouth confession is made to salvation and with the heart man believeth unto righteousness.**
> **(Romans 10:9-10)**

3. Accept the Plan and Purpose for Your Life Set in Motion By God Before the Foundation of the World.

> **A man's heart deviseth his way: but the LORD directeth his steps.**
> **(Proverbs 16:9)**

The steps of a good man are ordered by the Lord.
(Psalms 37:23)

4. Submit to the Lordship of Christ.
Submit yourselves, then to God. Resist the devil, and he will flee from you. (James 4:7)

5. Separate and consecrate yourselves for His Service.

I beseech ye therefore brethren by the mercies of God, that ye present your bodies a living sacrifice, Holy, acceptable, unto God which is your reasonable service, and be not conformed to this world but be ye transformed by the renewing of your mind, that ye may prove what is that good and acceptable and perfect will of God.
(Romans 12:1-3)

6. Seek Ye First the Kingdom of God, Not Things.

Seek ye first the Kingdom of God and his righteousness and all these things shall be added unto you.
(Matthew 6:33)

7. Pray, Fast, Meditate, Study and Seek the Face of God.

Eye hath not seen nor ear heard, neither have entered into the heart of man, the things which God hath prepared for them that love him. But God hath revealed them unto us by his Spirit: for the Spirit searcheth all things, yea, the deep things of God.
(I Corinthians 2:9-10)

8. Make your calling and election sure.

9. Do not procrastinate or make excuses.

10. Understand that there will be challenges, obstacles, and adversities.

> *We are not to be moved by what we see: for we walk*
> *by faith and not by sight.*
> *(II Corinthians 5:7)*

> *Ye are of God, little children, and have overcome*
> *them: because greater is He that is in you, than he that*
> *is in the world.*
> *(I John 4:4)*

Questionnaire

- Am I willing to stay in the House of God no matter how hard it gets?

- Is my foundation secure in Jesus Christ?

- Am I a hearer and a doer of the word?

- When God speaks, do I obey Him, trust Him, rely on Him?

- Am I respectful of the leaders within the church?

- Am I respectful of the person God has assigned me to serve?

- Is my relationship firmly established with the Lord?

- Am I making a conscious decision to fulfill God's plan?

- Am I willing to keep the commitment which I've made?

- Am I willing to be truthful / honest to myself and God?

- Am I being watchful, careful and prayerful at all times?

- Do I spend quality time in the presence of the Lord?

- Am I seeking God for direction and instruction?

- Am I acknowledging God's plans for my life?

- Am I Prayerful and do I walk in humility and extend love?

- Do I have a heart after God and for the leader?

- Do I know the vision of leader and my assignment?

- Have I yet spoken with the woman of God that He called me to assist?

- Are the lines of communication open with the leader ?

Chapter 4

God Has Plans For You

For I know the plans I have for you, declares the
LORD, plans to prosper you and not to harm you, plans
to give you hope and a future. (Jeremiah 29:11)

In Time All Things Are Revealed

Are you willing to allow the plan of God to come to fruition in your life? I'm not sure about you, but time and time again, I would ask myself what God's plan for my life was .The answer did not unfold all at once. As He slowly revealed things to me, I was led by God, step by step, to fulfill certain assignments. Part of His plan was for me to become a Personal Assistant to Lady White. Part of His plan was for me to write this book. Part of His plan was accepting not just the call to salvation but also to accept the call and responsibility of preaching the Gospel. Part of His plan was for me to travel near and far as a motivational speaker. Part of His plan was for me to serve within the Church in many of the ministries. As I said it didn't all unfold at once, but as it was revealed, He expected of me as He is expecting of *you* - to fulfill the responsibilities. God knows how much to reveal to us and at the appropriate time. He knows the beginning and the end, so it's important to believe the best way is *His* way.

I realized that many of my past experiences were preparing me for my future. Because God knows the plans that He has for you, it is up to you to seek Him and find them out. God will reveal His plan for you, with the intent that you will be in agreement and allow Him to bring it to fruition in your life. We are to trust God and know that he who has begun a good work in us is faithful to see that we complete it until the day of the return of Jesus Christ.

In order for God's plan to be effective, you must be willing to cooperate with him.

To everything there is a season, and a time to every purpose under the heaven.(Ecclesiastes 3:1)

When the season comes in your life for a particular plan to unfold, cooperate with the season. Allow God to demonstrate His power in whatever He wants you to do.

"For I know the plans I have for you," declares the LORD, "plans to prosper you and not to harm you, plans to give you hope and a future."(Jeremiah 29:11)

Remember these things:

- God said **I know**, the *plans* which means we have to find out not the plan but the *plans!*

- Do not put limitations or boundaries on God.

- God plans to prosper you.

- God plans not to harm you.

- God plans to give you hope .

- God plans for a future.

As in the natural, so in the spiritual, your cooperation is essential.

Picture this:

- Walking in the snow with flip flops

- Walking in the severe winter without a coat

- Walking in a 100 degree hot summer day with a fur coat

- Walking in the rain without an umbrella

I'm sure you get the picture. You are refusing to cooperate with the seasons!

Your Training is Essential

Growing in God is a process that doesn't happen overnight. We have to be aware that training is required for what lies ahead. So while we are on our journey, here are some tips to help us along:

- Read the Bible daily.

- Study the Word of God.

- Pray Daily.

- Meditate daily on the Word of God.

- Submit to the Word of God and resist the Devil.

- Fast as led by the Lord.

- Establish a personal/intimate relationship with the Lord so that when He speaks you will know His voice and you will obey Him.

Do you believe we exist for a purpose and with a purpose? Let us seek God for direction. We are not here just to be here; Let us seize the moment and move forward to accomplish our mission. God has equipped us with everything we will need so that whatever He asks of us, it can be done. Don't want to rush it or force it, but wait on the Lord for the appropriate time.

Remember Your Purpose

Look at the life of Jesus: He was born, died, and has risen with purpose!

For unto us a child is born, unto us a son is given: and the government shall be upon his shoulder: and his name shall be called Wonderful, Counselor, The Mighty God, The everlasting Father, The Prince of Peace.
(Isaiah 9:6)

And she shall bring forth a son, and thou shall call his name JESUS: for he shall save his people from their sins. Now all this was done, that it might be fulfilled which was spoken of the Lord by the prophet, saying, Behold, a virgin shall be with child, and shall bring forth a son, and they shall call his name Emmanuel, which being interpreted is, God with us.
(Matthew 1:21-23)

For the Son of man is come to seek and to save that which was lost.
(Luke 19:10)

Let this mind be in you, which was also in Christ Jesus: Who being in the form of God, thought it not robbery to be equal with God; But made himself of no reputation, and took upon him the form of a servant, and was made in the likeness of men: And being found in fashion as a man, he humbled himself, and became obedient unto death, even the death of the cross. Wherefore God also hath highly exalted him, and given him a name which is above every name: That at the name of Jesus every knee should bow, of things in heaven, and things in earth, and things under the earth; And that every tongue should confess that Jesus Christ is Lord, to the glory of God the Father. (Philippians 2:5-8)

But God commended his love toward us, in that, while we were yet sinners, Christ died for us. (Romans 5:8)

For this purpose the Son of God was manifested, that he might destroy the works of the devil. (John 3:8)

Our attitude must be the same. We are here not to fulfill *our* plan and *our* will, but to fulfill the will of God. Throughout the Bible we read where men and women were chosen by God to fulfill a specific task. Let us not just *merely exist,* but seek God to fulfill *His* will. God who created you knows you better than anyone and it is clear that He knows why you are here. We've got to become our own private investigators, seeking, probing, looking and getting the facts so that when it's all said and done we are able to move forward knowing God is well pleased because we are adhering to His call.

You might be the next president, pastor, prophet, prophetess, doctor, attorney, singer, judge, teacher or entrepreneur. Why not seek God in your pursuit? It is time that we stop wasting time, going around in circles and ending right where we started. Let us make some progress in fulfilling God's call in our lives.

God's Favor is Upon You - God extends favor towards his children. "God's favor" means that He will not allow our enemies to triumph over us! Hallelujah!

We walk in victory.
(Psalm 41:2)

In the case that you are feeling stagnant, prohibited, inferior, have become weary, thinking you can't do what God has called you to do, remind yourself and speak the words from Luke over and over again:

With God nothing shall be impossible.
(Luke 1:37)

Keep trusting in God and acknowledge him, He will direct your path. His favor doesn't mean that there will be no tests, no trials, no temptations, no adversities, *but it does mean no defeat.* Let us not live beneath our privilege, trying to fulfill the plan on our own, *but rely on God to show us how.*

God is your refuge, strength and present help in time of trouble.
(Psalm 46:1)

I am aware that the term "favor" is used very lightly today in modern vernacular but allow me to define favor according to the Merriam Dictionary. It means:

"Friendly regard shown toward another especially by a superior; approving consideration or attention; partiality, leniency, permission, popularity; gracious kindness; to bestow a privilege upon; to treat or regard with friendship, approval or support. "

Isn't it good to know we have all these benefits with the Lord? Yes, rest assure that we have favor with God and with men. God desires for us to prosper, to be in health even as our soul prospers.

The Bible says that we will know that we have obtained favor from the Lord because he has not allowed our enemies to triumph over us. Hallelujah! With His favor we are capable of withstanding the vices of the enemy.

God's favor is not seasonal; It is eternal. God is immutable, He is the same yesterday, today and forever, He doesn't change. His word doesn't change. He does not neglect us in any way, but shows his favor to us on a daily basis.

The Word of God says:

All things work together for the good of them that love the Lord and are called according to his purpose. (Romans 8:28)

Even the things we don't always understand, God can work in our favor.

Be Selfless Unto God

Having grown up with a strong, well-rounded Christian mother (whom I would consider my hero) and seven biological sisters, I know the importance of sisters being united and not divided, of our standing together and not fighting. Although we were all different in character, we had many opportunities to share our strengths, courage, support and love with each other and it was phenomenal.

As sisters in the Body of Christ, this is what it is all about. We are here to help one another. *As in the natural, so in the spiritual.* We need each other to survive.

It's time for us in the Body of Christ to come together and realize there no big I's and little You's. It's not about

40

you and it's not about me. It's all about us being united in God. With that being said, our primary purpose should be to please God. Too often we embrace knowledge but neglect to impart it. This is one of the purposes of me sharing. I am truly hoping that we can put our differences aside and see the greater picture. God needs us all to get out of our comfort zones and help someone else.

Whether you are assisting, aiding, helping or serving others, it's no easy task. Let's not kid ourselves. We know people are sometimes difficult.

I look back over my life and see how God was training and preparing me in my youth. In my community I would assist my mom as she would go here and there distributing food and clothing. I was able to watch as she helped to provide a safe haven for those that were without shelter. I didn't realize it then, but now I know that the Lord was shaping, making and molding me then for the present day.

The passion to help and please God during my youth and young adulthood has enabled me to overcome many obstacles.

In the chapters ahead there is a wealth of helpful information to assist you. I hope you will allow your spirit to be open and your ears attentive to the dynamics of serving. This ministry has allowed me to understand that "It's not about me." It's not about my plan, but God's plan. It is about me doing what he has called me to do.

There are many first ladies, prophetesses, evangelists, ministers and women in ministry who are in need of our assistance and there's a lack of women willing to make the sacrifice.

There are too many choosing to be competitive rather than learning how to be competent, too many wanting to serve for fame. There is a lack of support for the women in ministry today. Some women are comfortable doing for themselves and that's okay and that's their prerogative. On the other hand, some would permit others to assist if they would just step up. Why are we not working together? Far too many are trying to minimize someone else's ministry and gifts only to try and maximize their own selves! Sisters, our service must be about God.

It's always a good idea to re-evaluate what we are doing and why we are doing it. The conclusion of the matter should be "Lord, whatever you say, I will do and wherever you say go, I will go, because it's not about me, it's about working for you". We should begin encouraging our sisters to work for the Lord. We are one body, with many parts but the eye cannot say to the hand, I don't need you! Although we don't all have the same spiritual gifts, we should all be willing to serve for the same purpose - That is that God be edified, magnified and glorified.

Gifts and talents that you have comes from God and should be used to glorify God. We must make it our business to get rid of the "me" mentality and join the "we" mentality, for we are the Body of Christ. Let us not think more highly of ourselves than we ought to think regardless to the position and title we hold. We are God's servants, disciples and ambassadors. Let's make a difference by allowing the light of Christ to shine within us that others would see our good works and glorify our Father which is in heaven. God chose us! We didn't choose ourselves! Our primary purpose should be to fulfill his will. Whatever gift God has blessed you with, don't bury it, use it for not one gift from God is mediocre.

Some of the attributes (quality of characteristics) of an adjutant, armor bearer and personal assistant are patience and love. In addition, one's life should be consecrated. One should walk with integrity. One should have a consistent life of prayer and fasting along with grace, mercy and compassion. Assisting is truly about the Lord, Jesus Christ and not about you. Jesus said, "I came to serve, not to be served". Jesus helped those in need, by precept and example. Let us follow His example. He submitted himself to the will of God, the Father, even to death on the cross. Of course, there will be some who will serve for the wrong reasons, to be seen, heard, for name and fame. But consider again the life of Christ. When challenged with opposition, become optimistic regardless to what the situation looks like. Remember, we are spiritual beings. Therefore, we are not led by what we see, think or feel. We are led by the spirit of God who dwells in us.

God believed in you. He validated you when He choose you. Now is the time for you to believe in yourself and remember there is no turning back. Just focus on God and keep moving forward. The truth of the matter is it's about you doing what God has called you to do. One of the most important things for you to work on will be "attitude" - a "yes" attitude. We are to be a reflection of the Lord, remember "It's not about you; it's about the God in you." In all that you do in word and deed let it bring glory to God.

Assisting will bring many wonderful changes in your life so depend on God for guidance. With this assignment you will have both extensive and intensive on-the-job training, so learn from your experiences. If perhaps you feel unworthy or feel that you lack the qualifications allow God to perfect the skills within you and remember with God you can do all things. He will give you all the ammunition and fortification you need. Helping, serving and assisting, is not about carrying a Bible, driving first lady from church to church, or sitting in the pulpit to get personal recognition. It's about giving of yourself.

God has afforded me such a great opportunity and enriched my life through this assignment; the experiences were advantageous to me. This book will offer a variety of ways to assist and how to succeed as a result of your dependence and obedience to God. Throughout the book you will hear this repetitive statement "It's not about you; It's about the God in you". This is so that we are always reminded of who is in control! Giving of yourself is not as easy as it looks, but with God it can be accomplished. Reflect on this scripture:

I can do all things through Christ that strengthened me.
(Philippians 4:13)

Chapter 5

Adjutant, Armor Bearer and Assistant:
Your Call to Service

In any of the following capacities: please regard the following:

- You are an integral part of the body of Christ, used exclusively to assist God's Leaders. You must *have the heart of the leader*, be respectful and not a busy body.

- *Make the necessary sacrifices* to serve and aid in the spirit of excellence. This spirit will accommodate the leader on any given task.

- Serve as a watchman, being extremely attentive, listening for plots and schemes that may hinder or destroy the leader. Be the eyes, hands, feet and voice when needed.

- You are not the leader, but are subject to the leader. You understand and submit to delegated authority.

- You are not moved by what is seen. You are led by the Spirit of God.

- You must comply with boundaries.

- You must be teachable and accept constructive criticism.

- Support the leader in all aspects: physically, mentally, emotionally, spiritually and financially.

- Uphold and support the vision of the leader.

There are several roles within the ministry that need your help. Here are the definitions of those roles. Let's just review the basic roles and then we can talk about your place within this particular ministry.

Adjutant: To help; An assistant
(Webster's New World Dictionary and Thesaurus 2nd edition)

Armor Bearer
The armor-bearer (also spelled amour bearer) was a servant who carried additional weapons for commanders. References in the Bible to armor-bearers are Abimelech (Judges 9:54) Saul (1 Samuel 16:12) Jonathan (1 Samuel 14:6-17) and Joab (2 Samuel 18:15).

Armor-bearers were also responsible for killing enemies wounded by their masters. After enemy soldiers were wounded with javelins or bows and arrows, armor-bearers finished the job with clubs and/or swords. After the time of David, armor-bearers were no longer mentioned. Commanders began to fight from chariots (I Kings 12:18, 20:33) Today, we don't kill with bows or arrows. Our responsibility is to reconcile man back to God. With reference to carrying the armor, we do not take that lightly. Our armor now is the Word of God that heals, saves, delivers, makes whole and sets the captives free.

Assistant: Assisting; helping; one who assist; helper;
Aide, deputy, henchman, friend, follower, adherent, auxiliary, lieutenant, associate, companion, colleague,

partner, helper, apprentice, fellow-worker, secretary, helping hand, patron backer, body guard, aide-de-camp, ally, accessory, clerk, collaborator, confederate, mate, helpmate, right-hand, right-arm, friend in need.

(Webster's New World Dictionary and Thesaurus 2nd edition)

In any case as we serve and assist there are some important work listed below:

- Study the word of God.

- Apply the Word of God daily to your life.

- Be equipped for battle, by learning about the Armor of God.

- Be able to minister from all aspects: physically, mentally, emotionally and spiritually.

Below is a list of the outward attire the Roman soldiers wore to protect themselves. Symbolically we use this Armor to withstand the fiery darts of the devil.

Belt of Truth
Breastplate of Righteousness
Shield of Faith
Feet shod with the preparation of the gospel of peace
Sword of the Spirit that is the Word of God
Helmet of Salvation

Define each piece of the Armor and it's purpose

- Belt of Truth

- Breastplate of Righteousness

- Shield of Faith

- Feet shod with the preparation of the gospel of peace

- Sword of the Spirit that is the Word of God

- Helmet of Salvation

Although **Prayer** is not considered a part of the armor of God, it does solidify everything. So **pray without ceasing**!!

In today's vernacular we may not call ourselves Armor-bearers but our responsibilities require the same tenacity. We must be faithful to the call and prepared to do the job. We have the responsibility of serving physically and spiritually; we must be equipped for both. In the natural we must be physically fit for the battle and the race; so it is in the spiritual we must be spiritually quipped with the whole armor of God for spiritual warfare. (Prepared to counter attack the enemies schemes, wiles) The weapons of our warfare are not carnal but mighty through God to the pulling down of strongholds; (II Corinthians 10:4). Pursue your assignment don't allow the enemy to frustrate you:

- Stand your ground and do the work that you've been called and assigned (don't sweat it)! Things happened that I wasn't pleased with and wanted to say something about but I didn't, I had to press through the mess.

- There will be times that you are included and times you are excluded. People will do things out of spite trying to rub you the wrong way; but this is all apart of the character building and discipline. Continue to do the right thing. I confess, sometimes I took it personally because it was deliberately done, but I kept serving and praying at the same time, Lord help me to do the right thing, why? Because it's not about you, it's about the God in you getting the glory out of every situation. You will have to clear your head, think and behave rationally and not irrationally, this is what God expects.

- There may be occasions you will not be invited to. Find out what's what before you become frustrated.

- If you know that someone is intentionally doing something towards you with regard to your assignment, speak with them to resolve it. Don't allow anger to build up. At some point you may find it necessary to discuss with the person you are serving.

- Some events are held in the evening and can be late. Ask your Leader if she would like for you to stay or if it is not necessary. Leave when she releases you.

- One final heads-up, although you think you may be the one she wants to assist her on all engagements, don't make that assumption. She may rather have someone else to accommodate her; find out. As her assistant you do not have authority to ask anyone to assist in your stead, or take upon yourself invite others to the engagements; consult her regarding both of these issues.

We do not carry the sword (weapon) literally but we do indeed carry "The Sword of The Spirit" The Word of God that minister's life - abundant life and eternal life. There is much more power in the Word of God than with the man-made armor.

The references below reveal the power that is in the Word and we possess this supernatural power. The WORD is our weapon to overcome and resist the enemy. The Word is what we use to fight the demonic forces. Although we are not out to kill anyone, this does not negate the fact that our leader's lives will not be in jeopardy at one time or another. People are bringing guns to church and robbing churches without remorse. Those who are in ministry are depending on us to some extent to be their personal watchman. What they don't hear and see, we do, as we depend and rely on God.

We live in a world that is chaotic and hectic, a place where everybody seems to think everything they do is right, which means our leaders are there to preach and teach correction and instruction. I'm sure you can witness to the fact that everyone that enters the church isn't coming for the right reason, and everybody will not accept the truth. Some folk will get mad and literally act out. It is the Word of God that will set captives free, not guns and knives. We are not there to bring forth physical death but spiritual healing, life and peace through the word of God. No javelins, bows and arrows can do what the word of God can do.

Finally, be strong in the Lord and in His mighty power. Put on the full armor of God, so that you can take your stand against the devil's schemes. For our struggle is not against flesh and blood, but against the rulers, against the authorities, against the powers of this dark world and against the spiritual forces of evil in the heavenly realms.

Therefore put on the full armor of God, so that when the day of evil comes, you may be able to stand your ground, and after you have done everything, to stand. Stand firm then, with the belt of truth buckled around your waist, with the breastplate of righteousness in place, and with your feet fitted with the readiness that comes from the gospel of peace. In addition to all this, take up the shield of faith, with which you can extinguish all the flaming arrows of the evil one. Take the helmet of salvation and the sword of the Spirit, which is the Word of God. (NIV - Ephesians 6:10-17)

With the Word of God we tear Satan's kingdom down. You are there to pray and intercede on their behalf, praying against principalities and spiritual wickedness in high places. You are decreeing and declaring there is no weapon that is formed against them that shall prosper.
(Isaiah 54:17)

Man shall not live by bread alone, but by every word that proceedeth out of the mouth of God. Matthew 4:4

For as the rain cometh down, and the snow from heaven, and returneth not thither, but watereth the earth, and maketh it bring forth and bud, that it may give seed to the sower, and bread to the eater: So shall my word be that goeth forth out of my mouth: it shall not return unto me void, but it shall accomplish that which I please, and it shall prosper in the thing whereto I sent it (Isaiah 55:10-11)

For the word of God is quick, and powerful, and sharper than any two-edged sword, piercing even to the dividing asunder of soul and spirit, and of the joints and marrow, and is a discerner of the thoughts and intents of the heart. (Hebrews 4:12)

Remember you are there to assist, aid and help. We are women on a mission! We are praying that the word convicts, saves, heals, cause the deaf to hear, lame to walk, blind to see. We are praying for the people to be filled and re-filled with the Holy Spirit. We are women who not only see a need but are willing to support the need. We are women in ministry called by God to fulfill His plan in our lives. We are women who will not back down or take down. We will push, press and progress in God's plan. We are women willing to support in whatever area of ministry that's needed. We are women who believe in the power of prayer and faith. We are women who believe in one another. We are women who stand united. The Word of the Lord declares that one can chase 1,000 and two 10,000. (Deuteronomy 32:30). We are women chosen by God for a divine assignment! My dear sisters your labor is not in vain.

David was a prudent man, a mighty man of valor, a man trained, skilled, and a man of war. When he killed the lion and bear, it was preparation on how to kill Goliath. As he took care of the sheep, he was being groomed, trained and prepared to be appointed King. David knew the victory was his because God was on his side. He used natural items, but it was truly a supernatural power that brought forth the result! A slingshot, smooth stones and faith in God to kill Goliath! David was skillfully trained by God how to lift the evil spirit off Saul. He was a man that was led by God although he didn't make all the right choices and decisions. No, he didn't dot every "I" and cross every "T" but he had a heart to please God. This is the heart we should have, a heart to please God.

And David came to Saul, and stood before him: and he loved him greatly; and he became his Amour

Bearer. And Saul sent to Jesse, saying, Let David, I pray thee, sit before me; for he hath found favor in my sight. (I Samuel 16:14-22)

From the above text it is clear that David wasn't looking for an *assignment he was chosen because God trusted him. David used his gifts for the glory of God.* You may have a gift that is being over-looked right now, but wait, because God will allow someone to seek you out as He did with David. It is clear that he was a man of God and that the Lord was with him. I believe God has equipped you with the gifts for this ministry and He holds you accountable to serve for His glory. David was being trained for the assignment before he was actually appointed to the assignment. He was learning skills and being trained to be patient, compassionate, wise and hard working, while attending the sheep. No doubt this took much time, dedication, faithfulness and sacrifices; it was hard work, perhaps even a job no one wanted. All of David's gifts and talents were culminated together to do a great work for God. Not only was he called upon to minister with the harp but to serve as Saul's Amour Bearer.

I imagine David playing for Saul was like that of today during our Praise and Worship Service. People coming in bondage, weak, burdened, heavy, pain, sickness, diseased, troubled and most importantly, in need of salvation. They are strengthened and encouraged through songs of praise and through the preached word. The Lord has anointed you to do the same. Look around and see the Power and Presence of the Lord is alive and actively destroying the yokes of bondage, lives are being transformed and reformed.

When you feel like you're not qualified, remember *God chooses whom He uses.* He used Rahab who was a harlot because she was willing, He used Saul, who was once a murderer; because he was willing. He will use you; He wants to use you; are you willing?

For I am the least of the apostles, that am not meet to be called an apostle, because I persecuted the church of God. (I Cor. 15:9)

Effective ways to minister to the leader:
- Seek God's guidance and obey Him.
- Ask her to share her vision and submit to her.
- Become a faithful prayer warrior and intercessor.
- You are there to assist, help, encourage, uplift, pray, be a friend, be supportive and attentive to her personal needs.
- Show genuine love and concern.
- Make a difference, do what's best at any given time.
- Give godly advise and not your personal opinion.

Effective ways you can encourage the leader:
- Send a card, flowers, fruit basket an e-mail or go out to lunch to celebrate her birthday, mother's day, Christmas.
- Periodically call to be sure she is well and if there is anything you can do for her.
- Be there when she needs you.
- Always encourage your leader. Remind her of the promises that are on the way.
- Keep her reminded you are her keeper, you got her back.

The Lord impressed in my spirit the "JB" method; that simply means "Just Because" with no strings attached, no special celebration or event!

- Send a card, email, text,

- Bouquet of flowers, Edible Fruit or go out to lunch
- Put a little cash in her hand, purse or Bible

As you have been called, anointed and appointed to this assignment, give it all you got. Be effective and efficient. It is suggested that while on this journey you retain a personal guide; simply gather information that you believe will be beneficial. A outline is listed below:

Keep a list of Personal Information:

- Emergency contacts—husband and children
- Date of Birth
- Allergic to foods and or medications - including over the counter Medical History in case of an emergency (hypertension, diabetic etc)
- Medication and or Dosages
- Over the counter vitamins
- Hospital preference
- License plate number - be sure it is not expired
- Types of foods and drink she likes
- Favorite Restaurants
- Favorite Flowers
- What kind of entertainment she likes
- Clothing and shoe size and favorite color
- Special friends for special events

Chapter 6

The Dynamics of Assisting:
Guidelines, Attitude, Challenges and Helpful Tools

It is vitally important to know when, where and how to serve your leader. Therefore, you should be attentive, assertive, sober and vigilant. Study your leader to better serve in the capacity to which you are called. Pray for a sensitive spirit to the Spirit of God as well as the leader of God. Stop, look and listen to what is said and what is done. This way you will be better prepared to serve. Look at gestures, facial expressions, style of preaching; what comes next - the formalities if you will. If you have any indication something is not right, pray immediately and depending on how serious it is, make direct contact with her. You are to be on guard, a watchman, and her under-girder. Take notice of your surroundings (entrance, exits) and the people.

After she preaches, try not to allow folk to enclose her all at once. This can be a bit overwhelming especially after coming down from an exceptionally high service in the Lord. Try to stay focused and not become distracted so easily, because you are there to serve.

There will be some things you experience that do not make sense at the time; but just know that God is working.

And we know that all things work together for good to them that love God, to them who are the called according to His purpose.

(Romans 8:28)

God has it all under control. He is the ruler of everything. Whether you are assisting her at churches or any affair, if you are not "at home", be respectful of the people who have invited her and by those in charge. It is socially unethical for you to make decisions at someone else's house. This will also help to avoid confusion.

If possible, try to be within her line of sight in case she motions for you to assist her. There are seats that may already be delegated to others who will be attending. Remember your role is to serve her. It is the responsibility of the leader to speak with those in charge if questions arise unless she asks you to do it for her. If not, simply be still.

Sisters, there are so many women traveling alone. We not only need to make ourselves available for traveling, but willing to encourage, strengthen and undergird them. We need them and they need us. We need to join in as one body, fit together, not envious or jealous, but available to serve. We should support and pray for each other. Women of God, be sure you know God has appointed you to serve and make up your mind to be faithful and trustworthy. There will be many opportunities to share and embrace thoughts and ideas. Stay open to hear and receive these opportunities. Remain steadfast under pressure. Become an intercessor. Seek the Lord daily and listen attentively to the voice of God.

General Guidelines for Ministering and Assisting Others

Ministering: verb (used without object) To give service, care or aid; attend, as to the wants or necessities. (Roget's Dictionary)

- The Holy Spirit has anointed us to set the captives free. He will also teach you how to walk in your God-given assignment

- Pray for guidance and discernment on how to minister effectively.

- Where problems arise, seek God to help you discern the root cause.

- Always consider yourself before ministering, so that you minister with the spirit of humility.

- Remember that you do not have all the answers, so work together to resolve the situations.

- Always be willing to acknowledge your own sin. Be willing to cast out the beam out of your own eye and then you will see clearly to cast out the mote out of your brother's eye.

- Confess your faults one to another and then pray for healing, forgiveness and seek peace.

- Let the Word of God be the final authority, not your own ideas or thoughts.

- Be reasonable and teachable.

- Don't regard iniquity in your heart. Let it go. Keep God's Word in your heart that you might not sin against him.

- When you are challenged or faced with something you do not understand, always pray. Be quick to hear, slow to speak and slow to wrath. Wait on the Lord; He will direct your path.

Attitude and Character

In our quest to assist, aid, and help one another especially God's Leaders, we must remember Jesus Christ, our Lord and Savior came not in the world to be served but to serve. It is with this unselfish spirit that we should strive in our representation of him.

God so loved us (the world) that He gave His only begotten son, (Jesus Christ) that whoso ever believeth in him shall not perish but have everlasting life.
(John 3:16)

In everything we do and say, we must always remember to keep Jesus our focal point, He is our prime example. It's imperative that you learn how to serve by studying the life of Jesus, and then making application of it. As born again believers, our mission is to be a doer of the Word and not a hearer only. We must practice what we preach and practice what we have learned.

This brings us to a place of spiritually maturity. People watch and listen to you so let your light shine and live so that your life pleases the Lord. Try to make it a point that what you do and say is supported by the Word.

A servant's heart should possess these qualities: passion, compassion, grace, mercy, a readiness to give the benefit of the doubt instead of condemnation because with the same measure of long suffering and mercy we give, we receive. It's a good idea to have an optimistic attitude. You should earnestly desire to acquire an authentic heart of a servant. Your will should be to do the will of the Father. The way your heart is will be relative to the way you act. In other words, what's in your heart will be exposed.

I recall having to go to New Haven with Eldress White where she preached at a woman's service the Pastor said, you are transparent, you can see the love and support that you have for the woman of God. He said it was simply phenomenal to witness.

Although we live in a self-centered society our ultimate goal should be to assist one another and get rid of the self centered mentality. Jesus was not self-centered. Nothing he did was for himself. He died for us!

You are to be humble and willing to conform to the Word of God and not your own reasoning. You are not to be high minded, proud or boasting about your gifts or abilities because they all come from the Lord. The only thing we can boast about is the God we serve. Our attitude and character should exemplify Him. When we speak, we should speak the truth in love, not be a judge or one who condemns. It is the power of God that transforms lives. I believe within our hearts and minds we should sincerely strive to please the Lord.

Trust in the Lord with all your heart and lean not to their own understanding; in all you ways acknowledge Him and He shall direct your path. As the scripture teaches man plans his ways but the steps of a good man are ordered by the Lord.
(Proverbs 3:5-6)

I encourage you not to be moved by the faces or voices of the people. Know *who* you are working for and work faithfully.

Learning how to serve is vital. Pay attention when she preaches or is the facilitator for women's conferences. Consider what contributions you can make to improve and help the ministry be more effective. Examples might be altar work, preaching, teaching, exalting, or ministering with song.

The faithful servant must be reminded that frustration, discouragement, disappointment, jealousy, misunderstandings are all tactics used by the enemy to force you out of God's will. Remain faithful. Keep serving even under pressure. Do not subject yourself to the Devil. He is not your master. God is in charge of your affairs. He called you to do His will. Keep in mind that you are to be attentive, sensitive, watchful and aware of the surroundings and last but certainly not least, led by the Spirit that will make serving easier.

Allow serving others to be a priority in your life just as Jesus did. We must grow in the knowledge of our Lord and Savior then we can do as he did. We are to employ ourselves for the work of the Lord.

Let's review the fruit of the spirit.

But the fruit of the Spirit is love, joy, peace, long suffering, gentleness, goodness, faith, meekness, temperance: against such there is no law. And they that are Christ's have crucified the flesh with the affections and lusts. If we live in the Spirit, let us also walk in the Spirit.
(Galatians 5:22-25)

It's not what you say, it's what you do! Actions speak louder than words. The fruit of the spirit consists of various character qualities (frame of mind, personality, spirit, disposition, and make up) and attitudes that are a result of being filled, directed and empowered by the Holy Spirit. We must build and work on these characteristics in order to serve in excellence; what will remain afterwards is evidence of a heart of a true servant.

The Fruit of the Spirit:

Love	Goodness
Joy	Faith
Peace	Meekness
Long Suffering	Temperance
Gentleness	

Ye call me Master and Lord: and ye say well; for so I am. If I then, your Lord and Master, have washed your feet; ye also ought to wash one another's feet. For I have given you an example, that ye should do as I have done to you. Verily, verily, I say unto you, The servant is not greater than his lord; neither he that is sent greater than he that sent him.
(John 13:13-15)

For, brethren, ye have been called unto liberty; only use not liberty for an occasion to the flesh, but by love serve one another.
(Galatians 5:13)

Attitude is extremely important. Our attitude should depict Christ. Sometimes it's not what you say but how you say it. Other times it's not how you say it, but it's your body language that speaks it.

Consider the definition of Attitude:

Attitude- A manner showing one's feelings or thoughts; one's disposition, opinion, a quarrelsome or haughty temperament or manner. (Webster's New World Dictionary and Thesaurus)

- What is your attitude like when you are lied to intentionally?

- What is your attitude like when people talk about you? The world says, sticks and stones may break my bones but names will never hurt me. Sometimes we use words for that very purpose, to tear down and destroy.

- How do you react knowing you're being mistreated?

- How do you act when you are rejected?

- How do you act when you have been misused?

- How do you react when you are overlooked?

The primary characteristic of a Christ-like attitude is **"Self Sacrifice."** Jesus lived his life in complete selflessness. While we were yet in sin, Christ died for us. Are you getting the picture that it is really not about you? Anything less than a Christ-like attitude is self-centeredness. A self-centered person brings no glory to God. We've got to keep doing right in spite of the wrong that is done to us. When you do, it shows evidence of spiritual growth.

Visible evidence means that you truly represent God in word and in deed. In order to properly respond to His plan and purpose for your life, you must respond to Him through an attitude of Love.

The attitude of the old man (carnal mind) will not easily yield to do what is right. You must take control

*of it. Submit yourself therefore to God, resist the devil
and he will flee from you.
(James 4:7)*

The attitude of the new self (the spirit-controlled nature) is tempered with humility and truth. We have to put off the old man which is corrupt and be renewed in the spirit of our mind; and put on the new man, which after God is created in righteousness and true holiness. A Christ-like attitude is sensitive to the Holy Spirit who dwells within, because we are his children we are led by him and not ourselves. God doesn't want to reform us, God wants to transform us by the renewing of our mind, which is only available through Jesus Christ. God's goal is total metamorphosis. The only thing he wants us to do to self is die to self and live in Him.

*Remember your good is not good enough without
God. He knows the sincerity of the heart, the mind and
the motives behind our actions
(Isaiah 64:6)*

Once again I submit to you that your attitude toward leaders should be that of our Lord Jesus Christ. The love that God and Jesus Christ exhibited was love personified. It was indeed "Agape love."

Chapter 7

Ministry Beyond the Sanctuary

Serving and Assisting isn't just at the Sanctuary or at Your Leisure

The Loss of a Family Member

I didn't just serve Sister White in the Sanctuary. I served her personally. One of the toughest times was when her mother, Mother Elise Leaphart entered her eternal home. Sister White had to make plans, and I was there to see that what she desired was done. Sister White was called by the Hospital in South Carolina, because her mother had become ill while on vacation as she was celebrating her 70th birthday. I will always remember this because Sister White stated her mother's desire was to live until 70. The hospital requested Sister White's presence immediately. What devastation to arrive only to hear that her mother had departed.

I went to the house to make sure everything was in order and she soon returned. The pain of her sorrow was beyond words. There seemed to be no end to the phone calls or visitors paying their respects. I recall Bishop White sitting there at the table taking in call after call after call. You could visibly see the wear and tear on their physical bodies. I thought, people really meant well, and they were truly concerned but death is an overwhelming time.

I assisted so that she had as little stress possible. I prayed with her and for her that God would comfort as He promised He would. I would go to the house daily to handle whatever business that was needed in addition to cleaning, cooking, taking phone calls and assisting with the arrangements. During the home going celebration I was honored to expedite the service; as Sister White wanted to be sure it was not lengthy and ran as smooth as possible. This was truly an overwhelming experience for the family.

Sickness in the Family

On another occasion, Bishop White called and said "Sister Missy, Sister White is in the hospital." I said, "Bishop, I am on my way, but I need to talk with my husband." My husband said "Deb, go ahead."

I laugh now thinking about how fast I packed my bag. My husband and I agreed I could stay until she was released. Bishop does not like hospitals so I got there as quickly as I could. He stayed long enough to know what had to be done and he was gone; but he didn't have to worry because her "side kick" was right there by her side from the beginning to the end which was approximately ten days.

The doctors informed her of what was wrong as well as a solution, angioplasty to unblock her arteries. She looked so despondent; It's emotional writing about it even now. At that time I had a different perspective. I was on an assignment and had no time for crying or being passive. It was time to pray.

Of course, you know when you go to the hospital they ask who you are. I told them I'm her personal assistant. I will be sure to take care of her personal needs. I walked in her room and said "Hey, I'm here!" Of course she said "Sister Missy" I would do the usual and say, "Sister White". Bishop said, "I'm leaving". I just chuckled and said "See ya! You don't have to worry. I will be right here." I called home regularly to check on my family and my husband encouraged me that all was well at home.

Right now, I want to take this moment to not only reflect on Sister White, but to give God praise for my husband! I Love you, Woodrow and I thank you for being a man of empathy and a true man of God. My husband could have said no but he said "Go! We'll be alright." He took care of our house while I took care of God's business and our home did not go lacking.

If possible, no one should go to the hospital alone. You never know what's going to happen. In this case the hospital was overcrowded and they put Sister White on a psychiatric floor. People were hallucinating, trying to jump out of windows, yelling, screaming, and putting feces on the walls. It was a mess. In the midst of all that, the hospital staff wanted me to leave. They made an announcement visiting hours were over.

(Bishop said, "Well, Sister Missy, I guess we have to go." I said," Oh no, Pastor! I will not be leaving." He argued about the fact that they had asked visitors to leave but I politely asked him to please let me handle this. I reminded him that the hospital was placing her in room on the psychiatric floor and that I would not be leaving. I wasn't there for a visit. I was on an assignment, there to stay until she was released. I came prepared to stay with my bag packed. I proceeded to the nurses' station in a professional manner and asked to speak with the head nurse. Well, of course the young lady said that the head nurse was not there. I asked that they please call her because I need to speak with her immediately. She wanted to know what the problem was. I responded that there was not a problem but that I would not be leaving Sister White alone simply because visiting hours were over. I was her personal assistant. I then told her that I would happily wait for the head nurse. I politely asked her to contact her superior; I reiterated my purpose and what I would be doing; I would be staying with Sister White until she was released. I wasn't rude, but firm and wanted her to have a clear understanding as to why I was there to watch, pray and assist the Woman of God. Well, come to find out *she* was the one in charge!

Thank God she had a bed to sleep in. I had a chair and my black coat. I pulled my chair up on the side rail. We held hands, prayed every night and like a child, who was exhausted, fatigued and tired, she would fall fast asleep. I'd wrap my black coat over my legs, sit and watch her throughout the night. Although I had little sleep, God gave me strength. I felt rested every morning.

Sister White had to make decisions quickly. I remember her looking so puzzled and unsure of whether she should have it the surgery or not. We began to talk about it and she said, "Sister Missy what do you think? I responded I have faith and I believe when you go in you will come out in the name of Jesus. I then said, Sister White, God is in control, trust him; I believe God will protect you and give the Doctors exactly what to do. Sister White and I prayed in faith for the doctors, nurses, anesthesiologist and everyone who would attend to her during the surgery. Praise God there were no complications during the surgery or afterwards.

That very night that the doctors insisted that I leave. They thought that we both needed rest and recognized that I had been there every night. They assured me that I could come back first thing in the morning. I knew I had to leave because they had to prepare her for surgery, but I tell you that morning came really quick and I went right back. Before I left, we prayed and I told her to have the surgery; "Trust God and He will bring you out." I went home and straightway into my secret closet I prayed and the Lord said you have given her the right advice, and the tears just rolled down my face. He assured me that she would be fine. I breathed a sigh of relief. There is nothing like hearing a Word from the Lord!!! Did He do it? Yes, He did!! Hallelujah!!! I knew that everything would be all right.

The next morning I got my children off to school and headed back. I was so happy to see her. As I sat at her bedside, she reached out her hand and said "I miss you" and I said "I miss you too." We were like two kids.

The time arrived and finally she was transferred to another hospital. During the course of her hospitalization, medications were consistent, in her weak voice, she refused the medication, but the nurse just kept insisting. Sister White was weak, feeling sick, incoherent, tired and couldn't fight, but I could so I took the necessary action, and reinforced her NO! No means no, she said no! I said it very firmly and the nurse left the room. I kept a log sheet of the doctors and nurses as they would enter the room and the medications that were administered to her along with the time. One nurse forgot to document the medication in her chart book and they were about to re-administer it, but I told them that they had only given it to her two hours earlier. The nurse became a bit argumentative. Nevertheless, I refused to let her administer it to Sister White again. She asked and who are you, I replied, her voice and anything else she needs me to be.

Later on after doing the vitals and going through her chart another nurse realized the error and acknowledged it. She came in and said, that I was right, that they had administered it to her, but it was not logged in the proper place. Of course, we know these things happen. This was prior to a shift change. Sister White's one question was could it have ended her life, or could it have done permanent damage. Well, we were both unsure but what matters most is God told me to keep a record and because of that, it was prevented. To God be the Glory, He had it all in control. Sister White would say you need to sleep, I'm not here to sleep I'm here to keep watch; I wasn't tired, God strengthened me. I remained with her for ten days in the hospital until she was released to go home. On any given time that she had an emergency and was hospitalized even for a short time, there I was fulfilling God's call. She would tell whoever was there, Missy will be here in a minute, and there I was.

Helping in Times of Joy

Trina, Sister White's daughter, was now ready to deliver her child. Unfortunately, Sister White could not stay with Trina because she was not feeling well. I was called to the hospital again and shortly thereafter was told that I was unable to enter the room delivery room. Well, I thought to myself, I guess I'll just have to climb the walls and enter through the window!

Finally, I got clearance to go up and Trina started laughing hysterically. She said, "Sister Missy, I didn't know what those people were talking about saying the coach was here but I thought in my mind that it must be Missy because my Mom had to leave."

As the time got closer Trina got a surprise visit from her husband James and son, Nooch who had been asking for his mom. As fast as they entered the room they made their exit out. James came in with the biggest cool-aid smile on his face, and said, "Hey Sister V. glad you are here. Gotta go!" We prayed for Trina, the baby, a speedy delivery, and for the doctors and assistants. Trina and I held hands and she began to push but the doctor realized that the umbilical cord was around the baby's neck. Immediately I began to pray for the baby's protection as well as for Trina. Within moments she was blessed with a beautiful baby girl, Janay L. Hairston, weighing 6 pounds, 10 ounces. God was not going to allow the enemy to abort His plan with this birth. I am so glad God gives us power and authority over the enemy.

Sister's, I encourage you to take pride in what you do for the Lord. Learn to be sensitive and passionate about your assignment. Count it as an honor and a privilege to serve the Women of God. Count it favorable that God chose to use you.

There is absolutely no need to become jealous. There are too many women walking alone and in need of an assistant. If this is where you belong, you will find yourself in the position doing what is called upon you to do.

The final question that you must deliberate on is will you be faithful until the end to perform the work of the Lord? Remember to keep God first and work faithfully for him.

Things to consider:
- Having a heart of a servant, not looking to be served, but willing to serve.

- Being committed, dedicated, faithful, and serving with love.

My daughter, Lo asked me if I ever got tired of serving, I told her no. She likened my work to that of being a maid, but I disagreed. It's a gift from God and I really enjoy it. She said, "I watch you come out every Sunday morning with Sister White, and I'm like.. Go Mom, that's what's up!" Then she asked, "What is it that you do?" I said, "Whatever needs to be done." In short, travel, assist on pulpit, help her in office, get dressed, buckle her shoes or take them off. Lo was taken aback.

"What? That is a slave. She can buckle her own shoes!" To this I responded, "Lo, this is what serving, helping and assisting is all about. It's not about you." She said, "Never mind, I don't want to do that." I further explained that whatever you do for God is not for show. You don't serve to be seen nor heard or to gain friendships. It's about humility.

Chapter 8

Personal Guide and Tutorial to Serving and Assisting

In this section I would like to cover a variety of opportunities to serve and conclude with specifics and pertinent information as to where, when and how from a personal perspective.

One thing is certain, when people know you travel with the Leaders, they watch you more than before. Therefore, your character should reflect Christ.

Your disposition should be honorable even when you feel you have the right to retaliate. Be consistent in your quest to walk in humility and show love.

As you assist your leader I admonish you to discuss in detail the specific areas in which she is expecting you to assist. At this point, you will know her position within the church body: Prophetess, Pastor, Pastor's Wife, Elder, Minister, Deaconess, Evangelist, Soloist, or Motivational Speaker. This will help you to understand her roles. The level of your service will depend on the type of ministry the woman of God holds.

Things to consider:

- Is she preaching a Sunday Morning Worship Service?

- Is she preaching for a Women's Day, Mother's Day or revival?

- Is she the facilitator for a conference; will she be

providing brochures, handouts etc.?

- Find out if the engagements are local, driving distance, or if it requires flying or even a train. You can assist her by driving; (pumping the gas when needed) assist with making travel (train, airplane) and hotel accommodations if necessary.

Most Women's Conferences require a registration fee, hotel accommodation etc. (Generally the church takes care of the itinerary, but it would be helpful for you to review the information with her). Usually the church will send her a combination of forms to complete prior to her attending the engagement. They generally will ask if someone will accompany her. Keep in mind that you do not want to become over burdensome with the expenses. Please be considerate and willing to offset your expenses should they do not deduct it from her honorarium. If you are willing to cover your personal expenses that should be discussed.

Discuss vacation schedules and times that you might not be available. This would really apply especially if you are also involved in the ministry at your church or in the community. Allow her to determine if she would like for someone to assist her other than yourself for that engagement; please do not take upon yourself to assign anyone. She knows you and you know her; you know how and the other individual may not know what, when or how to do what's expected.

Be prepared:

- To assist whenever and however you are asked.

- To preach in her stead in case she ask you.

- To give the response to a welcome address.

- To assist at the altar and pray.

Assisting her doesn't mean just to carry a Bible. It requires you to implement "The Triple-A" Alert, Attentive, Aware at all times. In addition it requires you to be sensitive to her needs. Utilize the gift of discernment; to be most effective in your ministry. There might even be a time that you have to be assertive, that too can be done in the spirit of love. People are not always polite, not always receptive to the Word of the Lord, you are not there for the people, but to be an example for the people and to keep her encouraged. If you happen to hear a complaint, remember you don't have to respond; everything you think is not expedient to be spoken and everything you do and say should be done decently and in order.

Luncheons, Conferences and Retreats

Things to consider:

- It is the responsibility of the Leader you are serving to give you directives. If you do not communicate you will encounter numerous problems. Consult with your leader before taking action into your own hands.

- It is in your best interest that you communicate to keep all situations under control. I encourage you to ask the leader what her preferences are so that you will do what she is expecting and not make an assumption to do what you think she wants. This will help you avoid much havoc.
- Prior to the services ask your leader what type of assistance they desire.

- Check with your Leader to find out seating arrangements; each engagement may require something different. She may advise you to ask the person in charge.

- If possible you should seat near the Leader so that you have good visibility and can serve more efficiently. Be sensitive to the Leader.

- Precaution, you may not have the opportunity to sit near, but try to make eye contact. If you have the opportunity go to her table and inquire if she is in need of anything; you can also come up with gestures that will indicate the need for her to see you; be as discrete as possible.

It might be as simple as giving her a fresh cup of tea,

or getting an item left in the car or the hotel room that she was going to distribute.

When she goes to the rest room, be sure you check out her hair, it's in place, her clothing, fixed properly. She could forget to fasten a button, slip hanging longer than skirt, clean nose, but not completely, skirt tucked up in her stockings, stockings sagging or have a run. (You get the picture, so many little things to watch out for) .

When assisting, we should try to minimize misunderstandings; it is advised to keep the lines of communication open. In essence this will be beneficial as to when, where and how you develop a foundation as well as a methodical way to assist her. You can't just start serving without some type of assessment to the needs of the individual. This will enable you to have clearer direction.

Things to consider:

- It's important to know the person you are serving because your expectations of her may be more than she is willing to do.

- Please do not expect her to act like you or do what you do.

- You need balance in the relationship and you need to know your role.

- You may expect your leader to say or do something that you deem as being in order because something was said or done out of order. She may or may not respond. You just keep right on serving and assisting. You and your leader are not the same nor will your responses be the same; just bear witness that Jesus is Lord of your life and let the light of Him shine forth. There are some leaders who are outspoken and some that are not, whatever the case God has called you to help, so just do that. You do not want to make a mess and have to clean it up. Some things are not worth a fight.

- Serving and assisting takes a lot of humility and sacrifices; it's imperative that you utilize godly characteristics; keep flesh under subjection.

Engagements & Preparations

Things to consider:

- Keep a calendar of the engagements and specify local or abroad.

- Pray before any travels.

- Inquire of what materials will be needed. (pamphlets, literature).

- There might be times when you think there is more you can do. Find out; don't hesitate. Please, please do not make assumptions. If you don't understand something, get clarity, communicate.

- Get a copy of her letter for engagements, contact person (s) and directions. Be sure to talk it on the trip with you. Sometimes the church sends out a questionnaire to better serve her; be sure to remind her to review it and send it in.

- Touch base with her a day or two before engagement

- Verify church name, date, time, city, state, location, direction

- Color scheme (Women's Day) and Theme (Scripture)

- Transportation (car—prepare to pump gas / train and or plane; assist with her luggage.

- Hotel name/directions with place and time of

arrival and departure. Assist in and out of vehicle.

- Keep an umbrella handy.

Church & Pulpit Etiquette

Things to consider:

- Announce her arrival to appropriate person.

- Look at the ladies upon entering the sanctuary, if jewelry is not worn, inform her and take them off (respect the house).

- Be aware of surroundings outside/inside.

- Quickly locate bathroom inside.

- Carry garment bag and Bible in and out of church.

- Take her Bible, purse and binder to pulpit; checkbook, ink pen (necessities).

- Pray before she goes out to preach; pray and remain prayerful during service.

- Before entering the Sanctuary look at her clothing (zip, button lap scarf, etc.) (extra change of clothing).

- All ladies do not preach from the pulpit depending on the church.

- Allow the visiting church to inform you where to sit, your leader may want to ask when you are in the office.

- Be prepared to serve as the personal pulpit attendant.

- Find out in advance what she would like to drink (hot tea with sugar, equal or honey / lemon etc. juice, water—cold or room temperature).

- Does she drink before, during or after she preaches?

- Be sure you have a towel/ face cloth for her face.

- Provide hand sanitizer, tissue, lotion, bobbie pens, clear nail polish, bandages, hard candy or mints.

- Carry an extra ink pen and extra cash/credit card or checks.

- Prepare to give response from the welcome address.

- Locate exits in and out, front, back and side of church.

- Always position yourself in a visual position for her to see you.

If while on the pulpit you notice something that needs to be fixed (her attire, hair, runny nose) get to moving as discretely as possible. It will be a good idea to set up a code so that she knows what you mean or vice versa.

Respect all churches you go to. All women are not permitted to preach from the pulpit or wear pants (keep a skirt in the car).

When you're helping, assisting and serving you want to keep things in proper perspective. If you are in other ministries within the church, keep them prioritized. Assisting in ministry requires patience and skill. When you assist you want to guard your heart from frustration.

You might consider keeping a journal. Familiarize yourself with how she allows God to use her in ministry. In her own unique way and with the leading of the Lord, each individual will flow differently in the anointing of God. If it's a conference you might find yourself handing out literature where as a Sunday morning you'll be assisting her on the pulpit, in the office, in the prayer etc. As there are a diversity of gifts there is also a uniqueness with each individual which will also require different ways in which you might assist. The main thing is that you serve as unto the Lord. If there is more than one that assist, then she might have a rotating schedule. During the engagements inquire and be clear if she is she requesting you to stay for the reception or if you are dismissed. Please don't try to overstep those in charge. If you are asked to leave, simply leave. I repeat again, it is the leader's responsibility to speak on your behalf. At a later date you should discuss in detail, the expectations of your leader because it could create unnecessary problems.

Be Alert & Attentive

Things to consider:

- Watch and pray when she's preaching.

- Be watchful! I remember on a particular occasion she was not feeling well; she didn't say anything. I knew by observing her gestures. I knew when the Spirit said pray, pray. It's important to hear when the Lord speaks. I recall clearly, The Holy Spirit saying pray!

- Be prayerful alert and aware at all times. Watch your surroundings, watch the people. If you're in the pulpit or in a seat, you are her supporter.

- Pray for the power of God to be released with manifestation of salvation, healing and deliverance.

- Stand up occasionally and encourage her, push her and pray for clarity of speech.

For as the rain cometh down, and the snow from heaven, and returneth not thither, but watereth the earth, and maketh it bring forth and bud, that it may give seed to the sower, and bread to the eater. So shall my Word be that goeth forth out of my mouth: it shall not return unto me void, but it shall accomplish that which I please, and it shall prosper in the thing whereto I sent it. (Isaiah 55:10-11)

- Be prepared to assist her in praying at the altar.

Sometimes God will sometimes speak to you in advance and sometimes, well, you just need to be prepared.

• Please respect the House of God. All churches do not function the same. If God gives you a prophetic word for the church, you are to get permission from your leader before you release the word to the church; your leader will speak with the Pastor of the house and determine whether it is to be spoken or not and know that your word should be judged. The Leader of the house will judge the word; speak it, allow you to bring it forth or say not at this time; whatever the decision, respect it. This is proper protocol wherever you are; even within your own church. On many occasions God used me under the prophetic anointing to speak a word to the Pastor, church and individually. I praise God because she know God had blessed me with this gift and allowed me to use it; yes she trusted me and I trusted God.

• Everyone that comes to church doesn't come with God in mind. There are all types of people in church: meek, weak, sick, addicted, frustrated, suicidal, an unending list; so when you are there you must be watchful and prayerful. Sometimes the Word would be going forth and you'll feel the forces of evil; pray until the anointing destroys yokes, struggles and strongholds. You have the power, use it. Read these scriptures: Isaiah 10:27 and Luke 10:19

Conferences & Seminars

Things to consider:

- Always keep watch and pray when she's preaching.

- Check with the woman of God, your leader, to find out seating arrangements. Don't just sit where she is, that might be the appropriate place, although she can suggest this to the person in charge.

- Find out if your leader is requesting you to remain after service. Some events such as convocations will not require you to remain.

Offering

You may be asked to assist with taking the offering, be prepared. Please bring an offering and some extra cash, check or credit card for emergencies

The Leaders Honorarium

Although they are most often taken, they can sometimes not reach her. I remember an offering was taken from a women's luncheon for her, but the love token was not given to her. Be on the lookout. We know they are not preaching for money, but they are worthy of it. I could not believe it. We discussed in detail from that point on that I would be sure to oversee and retrieve her monetary blessings and handle her personal affairs as needed (sign personal checks, fill out tax forms etc). The bible tells us in business be men, so I suggest that you too govern yourself accordingly. You take responsibility for receiving her offering once you go in the back and service has concluded. You do not want her just sitting around. If possible take her to the car, then go back to receive the honorarium.

If there are checks, do not sign without her approval. Do not go in her purse without permission. Remember everything requires approval. Do not just make assumptions for this or that; it's best to ask. If she wants you to go in her purse, wait until she tells you or if she desires for you to write out a check, and sign; it just wait. Do not fill out the 1040 forms unless you are asked by her and please do not disclose her personal information.

Personal Assistant

The position of a personal assistant requires a good relationship and open, honest communication. From my personal experience I've walked this journey for more than twenty years, to God be the glory. There were times when I did have to speak on her behalf to others, as fore stated, I was her voice, her eyes, her hands.... I was there to ensure that whatever she needed was fulfilled to the best of my ability. I praise God for grace, favor and developing tactfulness in handling situations that were of importance. You will find that when approaching others it is extremely important that you consider yourself first. I must say I didn't make a lot of noise, but my presence was known. Although I am now Co-pastor of Mercy Tabernacle my husband continues to say it's okay for me to travel with her on engagements. I can truly say, I love the call, I value my experiences and submit to God in fulfilling His will.

I've had the privilege and honor to serve in these capacities:

Adjutant
Armor Bearer
Assistant to Church Functions
Conferences
Seminars
Women Retreats
Pulpit Attendant
Personal Assistant
Intercessor
Traveling Partner
Personal Nurse while in the hospital

- Perfection and excellence are the spirit in which you should be willing to serve.

- I developed from hands on training. From greeting her to departing from her at the end of the day each event was a continued learning process.

- I've met many people, sat in various pulpits, assisted on various occasions and none of them were the same. As the saying goes, "you live and you learn." I praise God for spiritual growth and maturity that came as a result of assisting.

- There are many ways in which you can personally minister to your leader. The most effective way is to ask her what it is that she desires for you to do. (Get a clear understanding of her needs)

The way to accomplish these functions was seeking guidance from God and asking what is it that I can do to better serve. In addition, I prayed, fasted, interceded, considered her, encouraged her and became a friend. Took pride in understanding who she was and made myself available and accessible when needed.

As a Personal Assistant, Adjutant, Armor bearer below is a brief list of some things you should have access too.

Standard Personal Information Data

Emergency contacts—husband and children
Date of Birth
Medications and Dosage
Over the Counter vitamins
Hospital preference
Allergic to any medications
(Including over the counter medications, aspirin, cold medicine)
Allergic to foods
Medical History (hypertension, diabetic etc.)
License plate number
(We travelled to VA, with one that was expired-thank God for grace)
Preference of foods and drink she likes
Favorite Restaurants
What kind of entertainment she likes
Flowers and Fruit Baskets
Type of clothing, clothing store, size of clothing and shoes
Favorite color
Relatives and friends for special events
Basically, you should have an idea of her needs and desires

Incorporate the "JB" Method

The Lord has impressed in my spirit the "JB" method; that simply means "Just Because" with no strings attached. You do without expecting in return.

"Just Because"
Send a card, email, text
Bouquet of flowers / Edible Fruit or go out to lunch
Speak a word of Encouragement
Put a little cash in her hand, purse or Bible
Do something special for her on Birthday, Mother's Day, and Christmas
In addition, periodically call to be sure all is well and if she is in need of anything. Always remember your assignment, you are there to help, aid, support whenever she needs you. Truly a phone call can make a difference.

Things to consider:

- Establish a life of prayer and fasting to empower, enhance and enrich you for ministry. God will uphold, preserve and sustain you.

- Seek God for insight on how to minister effectively to the woman of God.

- Pray with understanding and pray in the spirit also.

- Pray and ask your leader to come into agreement with you.

- Pray with confidence knowing God will hear and answer your prayer.

The most effective prayer, is to pray the word of God,

it will not return back void. As a reminder, the word of God is quick and powerful, sharper than any two edged sword piercing unto the diving asunder of the soul and spirit and the joint and marrow and discern the intents of the heart. (Hebrews 12:4)

- Empowerment Scriptures - The Word of God is our most Powerful weapon

- Death and life are in the power of the tongue: and they that love it shall eat the fruit thereof. Pray it, Speak it over every situation, Meditate upon it, Ponder it, Believe it, Live it and expect it to happen because the Word Works!

- Pray with confidence, know that whatever you pray for God will hear, and because He hears the prayer, petition, and supplication He will answer.

Sister's you need personal quality time for refreshing: Time to pray, fast, meditate and time to hear from God.

Things to consider:

- The Word is our weapon to overcome and resist the devil.

- The enemy, our adversary studies our behavior, laying prey to attack us at our most vulnerable times, so be sober and vigilant. Stay focused, alert, attentive, prayerful and watchful. The enemy plans, plots, and schemes with different strategies to destroy us. He works through discouragement, frustration and being unfocused. (Be on the lookout!)

- Protect and guard your heart so that you can fulfill your purpose. Hide God's word in your heart so that you might not sin against Him.

- Remember, it's not who you are but whose you are, you are a child of God and He knows what you are capable of becoming, so stay in the Word, nourish yourself and grow. The Word of God is our spiritual food. It gives life.

- Man's mind plans his way, but the Lord directs his steps and makes them sure. (Proverbs 16:9)
- The steps of a good man are ordered by the Lord and He delighted in his way. Psalm 37:23)

- In your pursuit of God, refresh your passion, your love, your dedication and faithfulness daily through His unfailing word.

Personal Boundaries

Personal boundaries are guidelines, rules or limits that a person creates to identify for him- or herself what are reasonable, safe and permissible ways for other people to behave around him or her and how he or she will respond when someone steps outside those limits. (Wikipedia Encyclopedia)   Don't violate - Cooperate—The purpose of this section is that you and the person you are assisting try to establish a healthy relationship.   Many relationships are broken as a result of lack of communication and not setting boundaries

As helpers one of another, I believe we should establish some boundaries as we assist in ministry.   First and foremost we must always remind ourselves without God we can do nothing.   God called, chose, anointed and appointed us to carry out His assignment.

- Have you set boundaries?

- Do you see the need to incorporate boundaries?

- Are you willing to comply with the boundaries and respect one another?

- Have you discussed the boundaries in detail?

- When boundaries are crossed how will you seek out a remedy immediately to resolve the situation?

- Are you capable of differentiating ministry and friendship?

Things to consider:

- The Booby Trap (Offended). An offense can be extremely complicated (most offenses are not intentional) and attempting to straighten out the offense takes patience, understanding, honesty, an open ear to listen and a willingness to forgive.

- The intent of this is solely meant to help you in the event you are at this juncture and / or to assist you in taking preventative measures to avoid such occurrences and/or reoccurrences.

A relationship should not dissolve on the account of an offense, a misunderstanding or because of discouragement, frustrations and especially **pride**. Pride goes before destruction. **Admit you are wrong,** ask forgiveness and do what is right and pleasing unto the Lord. These are tools and methods used to bring division and ruin friendships and relationships. Remember a friend loveth at all times and stick together through thick and thin.

Things to consider:

- Don't give allegiance to the one behind the offense.

- He who covers over an offense promotes love, but whoever repeats the matter separates close friends. **Proverbs 17:9**

- An offended brother is more unyielding than a fortified city and disputes are like the barred gates of a citadel. **Proverbs 18:19:**

- A man's wisdom gives him patience; it is to his glory to overlook an offense. **Proverbs 19:11:**

If you hold on to an offense it will affect you: spiritually, physically, mentally and emotionally. From a sister to a sister, you can't always determine externally what's going on internally. I want to encourage you: if you're going through an offense or in the event you are challenged in the future, trust God and not your flesh. I encourage you not to throw in the towel; don't quit on God, keep doing what he assigned you to do until you are released, because it's not about you.

Forgiveness is not an option; it's a must, absolutely, positively a "must do." Un-forgiveness is a sin; it is a wicked device used by the enemy against the body of Christ causing discord. Don't pretend that you're not affected by an offense, but honestly deal with the situation.

• Ensure positive reassurance from personal offenses

In my heart I want to make every effort to conclude each experience with a positive reassurance of God's faithfulness, love, forgiveness, strength and God's power.

Questionnaire

Take some time NOW, pray in secret, pray earnestly and reverently. There are some questions that should be answered truthfully.

- Have you set up an appointment with your leader to discuss what God has put in your heart to do?
- If no, why not?
- If yes, are you clear on the expectations required of you?
- Are you keeping a journal of the changes that need to be made?
- Have you taken time to write out the do's and dont's?
- Anything requiring a change, are you willing to change?
- Are you willing to cooperate with the leader?
- Do you believe you have the heart of your leader?
- Will you speak the truth in love, when an issue arise?
- Are you willing to acknowledge what you have done wrong and work toward a resolution?
- Have you personally experienced any offenses with your leader?
- How did you handle them?
- Would you handle them differently now, or the same?
- How can you prevent offenses?
- Are you willing to put the past behind you and move forward?
- Do you have concerns about your responsibilities?
- Do you know what your leader is expecting from you?
- What are your personal concerns (that you have not shared)?

- Why haven't you shared them?
- Are you going to share them?
- Did you have open communication?
- Did you set boundaries and did you discuss them in detail?
- Did you both agree to disagree, yet maintain a healthy relationship?

Sister's we are charged to be faithful even in the midst of the storms in our personal lives. We are not exempt from tests, trials or temptations, obstacles or challenges. People might question your ability, but don't be moved by that; fulfill your mission. God is not looking for one with qualifications; He is looking for someone who is available, is that you? You don't have to seek man's approval, or validation; just start doing what you've been called to do. Whatever plan God has for your life, let Him do it. God knows what to do, when to do it and how. He just wants a willing vessel. It's important that you know who you are and know that you do not need any recognition or affirmation to do what you're doing. Just do what God called you to do.

Some of the things that irritated me was being lied on, people disrespecting me for no apparent reason, or people having an attitude because of the work I was doing. I'd share bits and pieces with my husband and he would say to me, "Deb, be quick to hear, slow to speak, slow to wrath. Don't become a part of the person's problem, become the solution." He said, "you can't deal with a surface matter unless you kill the root cause." I thank God for my husband because he bailed me out plenty of times. No not out of jail!! Out of situations. I had no problem defending myself, but I just wanted to do right and people have a tendency to take advantage of meekness.

Things to consider:

- Are you willing to stand when it seems like all odds are against you?

- Are you willing to endure being lied on, talked about?

- Are you willing to be persecuted for doing right?

- Are you willing to be rejected by man and remain faithful to God?

Successful Ministry Power Points - Communication

Communication: Is the process that allows people to know each other, to relate to one another and to understand the true meaning of the other person's life. Communication is a foundational demand for a healthy, successful relationship. We must learn to respect the opinion of each other. A successful ministry means having a direct, open and honest relationship with the person you are serving. If the foundation is based on those factors the relationship can be built. How well are you in communication with each other?

Enhance Your Communication Skills

Things to consider:

- Be quick to hear, slow to speak and slow to wrath. (James 1:19,20)

- Be open and honest.

- Speak the way you want to be spoken to.

- Be willing to speak the truth in love.

- Speak with meekness and a willingness to restore one another.

- Communicate regularly.

- Love (action speaks louder than words).

- Be sure that you understand what the person is saying.

- If necessary, explain what you think is being said for clarification.

- Know the facts, not assumptions.

- Ask for wisdom, as to how you should approach the situation.

Perhaps, you say, all this is not necessary, I am not insinuating that you put demands on your relationship, but with all due respect, try to keep your relationship healthy and positive.

Things to consider:

- Learn to respect the opinion of each other.

- Learn to accept each other for who we are and not what you want one another to be.

- Work on your character flaws. Daily search your own heart, attitude and disposition they play an important factor in ministry. Attitude and motives are important, so monitor yourself.

- Acceptance, doesn't mean, we agree with everything each other does or says. Perceptions and perspectives, may differ, but the bottom line is as a team we should be able to come to an agreement and work together for the Lord.

- Learn the character of each other. If one has erred from the truth as a minister of reconciliation, fix it. How? By restoring your sister in the spirit of meekness considering yourself. Speak to the individual as the spirit of God leads you. Speak the truth in love not anger, when one has walked in err or in need of restoration.

- As hard as you would like for the person to change, consider yourself and the changes that are necessary for your personal growth. Remember, the same God that works on you will work on her.

"Continuity"

You can successfully continue to assist, help and serve in ministry through dedication, commitment, faith, love, determination and being resilient. It takes "continuity", The attitude that says, No matter what, I will continue to persevere. I will keep moving forward. You must determine in your mind and spirit that you will be "resilient". You must stay focused, keep yourself on the right track. Do what God said to do and you will stay on track. There will be times you will have to encourage yourself and tell yourself, "No matter what" I'm going to do what God has called me to do. With such an attitude, no matter what comes your way, your spirit will keep telling you to continue.

God knows that a time would come that you will need to have this spirit. He doesn't want you to stop working for Him no matter what, so *__Encourage yourself in the Lord__* and remind yourself that God has begun a good work in you and He is faithful to complete it. He is working all things out for your good even when you don't see it or quite understand all that's happening. Keep in mind that any challenges that you are faced with, you have the power to withstand. Be steadfast and unmovable always abounding in the work of the Lord, for as much as you know that your labor is not in vain in the Lord. (I Corinthians 15:58) Make every effort to do the right thing.

"Confidentiality"

It is vital and of utmost importance that you establish confidentiality in your relationship. Whether you were spoken to directly or indirectly whatever you hear should be kept confidential. Taking the liberty of sharing what you've heard in confidence beyond the walls is unacceptable.

Sisters, when your assignment comes to an end, confidentiality should not be broken. If your relationship is broken your confidentiality should not be broken; whatever you shared should remain between the two of you. For a moment consider those personal or intimate details in a conversation, perhaps situations that you shared concerning your spouse or family. You were honestly seeking advice and now that the relationship is broken it gives you no right to violate privacy. The truth is you don't want to hear what you've shared with anyone and vice versa.

"Spiritual Refreshing"

We are not superhuman or super-spiritual. We need to seek God for spiritual strength. In I Samuel 30:6 it says, And David, was greatly distressed; for the people spake of stoning him, because the soul of all the people was grieved, every man for his sons and for his daughters; but *David encouraged himself in the Lord his God. (KJV)*

Things to consider:

- God is our refuge and strength a very present help in trouble.   Psalm 46:1(KJV)

- The Lord is my light and my salvation; whom shall I fear? The Lord is the strength of my life of whom shall I be afraid. Psalm 27:1(KJV)

"Love"

Maintain your Victory with Love. Most people have experienced some sort of hurt in relationships, whether it was biological, church family or true friend, but "Love" mends it back together, because it keeps no record of wrong doing.

According to the Word of God, LOVE is an action word. LOVE isn't because of what you have done or did not do, LOVE is unconditional. You've got to maintain your victory! Don't let circumstance dictate how you act, think first. Read I Corinthians 13:1-13 "Love is the greatest gift" and remember that "Love" covers a multitude of sin.

Personal Overview

Take a moment to list your areas of concerns for yourself

1.

2.

3.

4.

5.

6.

7.

Since you have acknowledged your personal concerns, let's take the next step together, Write out your concerns, then Look in your bible concordance and find scriptures that pertain to your personal situation. Get spiritual guidance from your leader, spouse, and friend. Finally, determine to deal with the root cause. The mission is not impossible. Set your plan in motion and know that it will be a process.

Ministry begins at home

Although God has called us to serve, assist, aid, and help those in ministry; it is not His will that we neglect our first priority, which is our family. You should not neglect your spouse, children or family to work in the ministry. Truthfully speaking, this is the groundwork for ministry. Working within your home.

Assignment Questionnaire - Walk in your assignment and fulfill God's will   Assignment: A position, post or office to which one is assigned. (Merriam Webster)

Things to consider:

- Did God instruct you to serve or is it a personal desire?

- What were the instructions God gave you?

- Are you carrying out the instructions?

- Have you spoken with the individual to regarding the call?

- What was the response after the conversation?

- You are certain God called you and this is not for personal gratification?

- Have you taken the time to watch so that you can learn from what you've seen her do and what you have heard her say?

- If she is not in agreement with how you're serving will you quit or will you stay?

- Have you had any training in assisting God's leader before now?

- What do you find to be the most complex situation ? Have you taken the opportunity to evaluate your strengths weaknesses?

- How would you handle someone openly making derogatory remarks regarding the person you are serving?

- How were you able to identify the needs and concerns of the leader?

- Did you understand that when you assist, it is all for the glory of God?

- Did you assist because no one else was available and she was your friend?

- Are you willing to support her financially?

- What changes do you plan on implementing if any?

Chapter 9

My Personal Biography

Deborah D. Vereen, devoted, proud and honored wife of Pastor Woodrow Vereen, proud mother of five and grandmother of six. Co-Pastor of Mercy Tabernacle Church Inc, located in Stratford, Connecticut. A native of Bridgeport, Connecticut. One of fourteen siblings, raised in Father Panik Village Housing Project where poverty, drug infestation and alcohol abuse were prevalent, along with prostitution, violence and crime; Father Panik Village, identified as "The Ghetto" took a life of resiliency and determination to survive. Although Connecticut was reported on national television as the armpit for crime and violence Deborah is not afraid to preach to those of her city because God rescued, saved, and prepared her as his prophetic mouthpiece to share His goodness without fear or compromise.

As noted in the Word of God, can any good thing come out of Nazareth? Yes indeed in 1979, Deborah experienced a transformation as she accepted Christ as her personal Savior under the late Bishop James Vereen. Deborah, affectionately called "Missy" was called out from the housing project and saved by grace through faith by the power of the Almighty God and faithfully served as a Missionary, Church Clerk, Board of Directors, Choir, Usher and devoted to street services within the surrounding community. A graduate of Foundation Bible Institute, Jamaica Queens, New York, under the tutelage of Dr. Edgar Lashley. Deborah a former entrepreneur of fifteen years as a license home day care provider; received her Child Development Accreditation from Housatonic Community College and was on the Dean's list.

In 1987, the family was led of the Lord to join Turner's Faith Temple under the leadership of Bishop John C. White. There she served as an Missionary/Evangelist, Minister, Elder, Children's Church Director, Board of Directors, Prison Outreach Ministry, Founder of The Big and Little Sisters and more until 2013.

January 2002, Deborah was ordained to an Elder under the auspicious of Bishop John C. White, Pastor, assisted by her husband, Elder Woodrow Vereen, along with Elder Gloria White. What an awesome day as she was privileged and honored to be vested in the liturgical ordination vestment by Elder Gloria White. Deborah's husband, children, family and special friends surrounded her with love. Deborah is no ordinary Adjutant. She epitomized what it truly means to have the "heart of a servant". As she answered the call, she served as Adjutant, Armor-bearer and a devoted "Personal Assistant" more than twenty years to Elder Gloria White, First Lady, wife of Bishop John C. White, who serves as the National Supervisor for Cathedral of Praise C.O.G.I.C. International. As previously mentioned, it's important that we learn from our experiences. Only God knows when He will elevate us to the place He ordained to fulfill His purpose.

September 2006, God permitted Deborah to embark on new season in her life. The Lord directed her to release a prophetic word into the heart of Prophetess Lounsbury where she and her husband Apostle Tom Lounsbury serve as the Pastors of Lighthouse Ministries. God sent confirmation to Prophetess Lounsbury. It was soon after that a new vision was birth: Women of Destiny. Prophetess Kathy Lounsbury, Pastor Mary Gardner and Elder Deborah Vereen began to work in unity. The Women of Destiny is a ministry that serves as a regional effort to minister to women for Christ bringing healing, unity and a true sense of direction to their lives. In addition, God allowed Deborah to preach at two churches for two consecutive years; Danbury Lighthouse and Charity Christian Center under the leadership of Pastor Lula Vereen.

March 2007, Deborah received blessings from her Pastor, Bishop John C. White, to bring to fruition the vision from the Lord.   The Serenity House of Worship, passionately called "The S.H.O.W" came to fruition. The vision is that all women become one in spirit.   God revealed there was a cry for help among the women. This vision was held within the home of Elder Deborah. Women came and were empowered; shared testimonies of   victories   and   many   have   become   ministers, missionaries and assistant pastors.

October 2008 through 2012, the Lord opened doors in Kalamazoo, Michigan where Deborah became a keynote motivational speaker for the Project Uplift Program under the auspicious of Monteze Morales, who serves as the chairperson.   The   program   is   designed   to   bring awareness on sexual issues.   Literature from the health department was provided as well as counselors from the health department who provided an overview of the people located in the Michigan area with HIV/AIDS and STD'S. The health department provided aids testing for those who attended and many partook in the testing with rapid results. Professional counseling was available on site.   The events were open to all ages, races, parents, high school youth, college students and the public. No discriminations.   At   one   of   the   seminars   all   three generations were present which was simply phenomenal to see. Many of those who attended received personal guidance and spiritual help. Deborah was able to teach abstinence from a biblical perspective. She shared how God loves them and that he desires holiness from all of us. She also spoke briefly on physical, emotional and spiritual healing.

Her service has been exemplified in her church as well as in the community. In 2010, Deborah received the Humanitarian Award from The Al-Aziz Islamic Center for her support in the community and has been a motivational speak for the event as well as the Save Our Babies Foundation, hosted by Brother Lyle Hassan Jones. She is the Office Administrator for Morton's Mortuary Inc. A licensed Notary Public for the State of Connecticut. She loves the Lord and is a servant at heart.

October 2, 2012, a meeting was scheduled with Bishop White to inform him that God counted us worthy to led his flock and expand the Kingdom bringing to fruition "Mercy Tabernacle Church Inc." It was some thirty plus years ago that God gave the name of the church to her husband Woodrow. While we waited for our transition we keep busy doing God's work. We learned how to work as a team; how to be dedicated and faithful to God and how to follow our leaders. We have served in the various ministries individually and together to mention a few: James Vereen Ensemble Choir, Deacon, Missionary, Minister, Elder, Outreach Street Services, Sunday School Teacher, Church Clerk, Prison Ministry; Board of Directors; Youth Ministry, Husband & Wife Ministry, Converts Ministry and the Leadership Council which was a combination of Elders, Ministers, Deacons, Missionaries and Deacons in training.

In Deborah's experience, the greatest lesson learned is that you must be a good follower to be a great leader and you must lead by example. You must be committed, faithful and dedicated to God first, and not neglect your family then work within the ministry. With the help of God we have made a vow that as God leads, we will follow. It has been difficult for both of us as far as the transition because we were members of Cathedral of Praise for twenty-six years. It was truly an emotional time separating from the people and the ministry. We continued carrying out our responsibilities until Sunday January 6, 2013.

Sunday, January 13, 2013, "Mercy Tabernacle" celebrated the grand opening. Pastor Woodrow Preach, "Steady As You Go" the text of I Corinthians 15:16-57. There was an awesome time in the presence of the Lord. The Tabernacle was packed like sardines there was no room in the Tabernacle as Deborah's families and friends shared this celebration and worshipped. They were excited about what God is going to do and ready to follow his guidance. Deborah and her husband, Pastor Woodrow give special thanks and praise for their children along with their wives, eldest granddaughter Keziah, their siblings and many friends who assisted them. They were right there willing to help in every way possible. Their first Bible Study was held Tuesday, March 5, at Comfort Suites in Stratford, with the lesson being "Feeding on God's Word". They do not want to become malnutrition saints. Mercy Tabernacle is building a strong solid foundation. The Kingdom of God is being expanded; the Word of God is being executed, God is being exalted, and the power of God is in full demonstration. Souls are being saved, recommitted, healed and delivered.

Sunday, May 12, 2013, Deborah preached the first Mother's Day Message, "The Virtues of a Virtuous Woman". What a wonderful celebrating! Deborah's mother was ushered into the sanctuary by granddaughter, Keya and grandson, Travis. What a momentous celebration! Mother Stevenson desired to be there to celebrate and God allowed it to come to fruition. As a reflective moment, it was mom who actually said to her daughter, you are going to marry Woodrow and so it was on October 17, 1981 the marriage vows were witnessed among 300 family members and friends.

All glory to God for the increase in membership as the body of Christ is growing at Mercy Tabernacle. While God continues to open doors for Deborah to preach she is most honored that her husband is right beside her and fully supports her as well as her gifted and talented children Keya, Woody and Travis.

Deborah has had the distinct opportunity to minister a word of comfort to more than 175 families within the past 8 years. In addition, she continues to preach throughout her community and the surrounding areas. God has favored her with two faithful ladies Betty Smith and Tina Maurice who so willingly travel and support her.